ten poems to change your life

ten poems

to

change

your life

ROGER HOUSDEN

HODDER
MOBIUS

A complete list of credits for previously published material begins on page 131.

Copyright © 2001 by Roger Housden

First published by Harmony Books in 2001
First published in Great Britain in 2002 by Hodder & Stoughton
A division of Hodder Headline

Published by arrangement with Harmony Books, a division of Random House, Inc.

The right of Roger Housden to be identified as the Author of the Work
has been asserted by him in accordance with the
Copyright, Designs and Patents Act 1988.

2   4   6   8   10   9   7   5   3   1

A CIP catalogue record for this title is available from the British Library

ISBN 0 340 82509 X

Design by Karen Minster

Typeset in New Baskerville
Printed and bound in Great Britain by
Clays Ltd, St Ives plc

Hodder and Stoughton
A division of Hodder Headline
338 Euston Road
London NW1 3BH

For Maria Housden

Acknowledgments

First, my gratitude goes out to the ten poets whose work is the core of this book. Every one of them has added a measure to my life in some way. Then, in the case of those who wrote in other languages, I owe thanks to their contemporary translators— Robert Bly, Coleman Barks, and Stephen Mitchell. Robert Bly, I owe you a special debt for introducing me to the work of three of the poets in this book. It was you, too, who introduced not only me, but an entire generation, to poetry as the preeminent language of soul. In this regard, your place in American letters is unique. Maria Housden, I could not have wished for a more reflective and insightful companion along the way. Your editorial contributions were invaluable. Lee Macey, your editing gave the book its final shape, and your insights into some of the poems opened depths in them that I had passed over. Your passion for poetry has left its trace not only on the book, but also on me. This book owes its publication to the faith and commitment of one person, Patty Gift, my editor at Harmony, and its final shape and symmetry to the care and acuity of Toinette Lippe. Finally, my gratitude goes to Kim Witherspoon for her support of the project from its very conception.

There will soon be no more priests.
Their work is done. . . . Every man shall be his own priest.

—WALT WHITMAN

Contents

Introduction

Good poetry has the power to start a fire in your life. The first poem in this book, Mary Oliver's "The Journey," begins like this:

> *One day you finally knew*
> *what you had to do, and began,*
> *though the voices around you*
> *kept shouting*
> *their bad advice . . .*

Even now, after hundreds of readings, this poem grabs me by the shoulders, shakes me hard, and demands I look again at how honestly I am living my life. Poetry like this is rigorous, demanding, ecstatic. Not just to write, but to read poetry like this can be a fierce and dangerous practice; dangerous because you may never be the same again. This is how Emily Dickinson described the experience of reading poetry:

> If I read a book [and] it makes my whole body so cold no fire can warm me, I know *that* is poetry. If I feel physically as if the top of my head were taken off, I know *that* is poetry. These are the only ways I know it. Is there any other way?[1]

Great poetry can alter the way we see ourselves. It can change the way we see the world. You may never have read a poem in your life, and yet you can pick up a volume, open it to any page, and suddenly see your own original face there; suddenly find yourself blown into a world full of awe, dread, wonder, marvel, deep sorrow, and joy. Poetry at its best calls forth our deep Being, bids us live by its promptings; it dares us to break free from the safe strategies of the cautious mind; it calls to us, like the wild geese, from an open sky.

Well and good, you may say, but few of us have ever had that elevating experience. The only poetry most of us ever read was in high school, and then because we had to. There is an aura of formality and high culture still surrounding poetry that can make it seem pretentious, and irrelevant to our daily preoccupations.

Yet, would you believe it, poetry is as alive today as it ever was. There are more poetry festivals and readings starting up around the country than ever before, and more people than ever are writing their own poetry. More than twelve thousand people attend the Geraldine R. Dodge Poetry Festival, the most vibrant of them all, which takes place every two years in Waterloo, New Jersey.

Then there is the poetry slam, a whole new style of poetry reading. Young people stand up onstage and in a style of delivery akin to rap, perform their own work in a limited time span of around three minutes. Several poets perform, and judges from the audience give them scores and elect a winner. The slam is poetry as performance art in a competitive setting. It's exciting, participatory, and sometimes the material is astonishingly powerful. Large new audiences are coming to poetry as a result of the slam phenomenon. The current national slam champion, a young man known as The Shane, delivers work that is as moving as any I have heard.

But there is another kind of poetry, as old as the human race; and this is the kind you will find in this book. In a direct and accessible way, this poetry gives voice to a spiritual reality that is beyond the copyright of any religion. It voices the longings of the spirit and our deep desires—the desire for meaning, for a life of passion and creativity, for a sense of belonging, for wisdom, and as always, for love.

Consider, for example, the work of Rumi, the thirteenth-century Persian mystic. Earlier translations from the original Persian are stilted, but more recent renderings by Robert Bly and Coleman Barks have given Rumi a huge international following. In conveying the spirit of Rumi's words through their contemporary poetic sensibility, they have made it not only accessible but also dynamite. Like thousands of others, I was stunned to discover that Rumi—a man of the thirteenth century—not only knew my heart, but had laid it bare on the page. Today, his universality speaks to people of all faiths, and even those with none. The poem of his that I have included in this selection touches a deep nerve in me. It begins like this:

> *Be helpless, dumbfounded,*
> *Unable to say yes or no.*
> *Then a stretcher will come from grace*
> *to gather us up.*

These words are the fruit of mystical experience, not religious belief or dogma. Twenty years ago, Rumi was known only in specialist circles. Now, through the medium of his contemporary translators, Rumi is one of the bestselling poets in America. His work is read at business conventions, church gatherings, conferences, and has been set to music by a dozen different composers.

The fact is that there are visionaries writing today, as ever. Their work, too, contains the kind of knowledge that the soul thirsts for. The soul wants heart knowledge, a felt sense of the truth that we register not just with the mind but with the body and feelings—with our whole being.

This is the kind of poetry that you will find in this book. It is timeless, which is why this selection is drawn from different centuries as well as from different parts of the globe. It is the living spirit you will find here. That is one reason—especially in a time when institutional religion fails to speak to our spiritual needs—why a great poem can open a door in us we may never have known was there.

We, as the reader, hold the key to that door. The key is our capacity to listen, to pay attention. ("Attentiveness," Simone Weil reminds us, "is the heart of prayer.") The essence of all poetry lies ultimately in the meeting of poet and reader; that is where it truly comes alive. Then, through that encounter, the poem can proclaim our fundamental belonging in the world. When the poet is reaching into territory that lies just beyond our conscious experience, we may shiver and not know why. We may not understand the sense at first, or even a second or third time; yet some tidal pull returns us to it again, and maybe again, till finally, perhaps, some magic slips open the knot, and we and the poem stand revealed. In this way, too, poetry is an agent of transformation.

A genuine poetry of the spirit also embraces matter. The poet praises and celebrates the world of things and living beings in ten thousand ways. "The other world" is right here, before our eyes. The poem takes the scales from our eyes and helps us see what was there all along. One of the poems in this book is Pablo Neruda's "Ode to My Socks." He writes two pages on the sheer pleasure and awe of contemplating a new pair of socks. Neruda's general body of work is full of the beauty and surprise of the ordinary. He wrote odes not just to his socks but also to a tomato, to his suit, to salt, to an onion, to a rooster, and even to ironing.

But why only ten poems? Why not twenty, or even a hundred? I have chosen ten and no more because I am not setting out to offer yet another anthology of poetry, spiritual or otherwise. There are only a few life themes that pursue us down through the years, and even these, as you will discover in these poems, are echoes of one another. It is these spiritual and existential qualities that I want to address in this book above all else. Ten poems of this caliber are more than enough for that. You could even compress their voices into the one command: Wake Up and Love! But something great would be lost then, and that would be the enchantment of the telling.

So this is a book that aims to alert readers to whisperings under their own skin, hunches in their own gut. It is not for poetry lovers alone, but for everyone who knows there is more to life than they are presently living. I intend it as a book of inspiration and awakening. The poems are the gateways for this, and they do of course stand on their own high merits. Yet they also serve as catalysts for the further reflections that follow each poem. These develop the life themes that course through the poem; and they provide a setting for your own responses to it.

Then why these particular ten poems, when so many others might have done just as well? Personal prejudice, no doubt, as with any collection. It is no accident that three of the poets are saints, and from three different traditions. The whole point of their writing—their teaching—was to turn others around. Then, I preferred to include contemporary poets and translations over those from an era whose language made them less accessible. I also wanted to avoid the English and Irish Romantics, because their work is available anywhere, not least in high school. Whitman is the one poet I have included from that time. I can't help it; I just love his brand of wildness, however familiar his voice may be.

The guiding light of my selection, though, is my belief that each of these poems has the power to change a reader's view of the world, and thereby, their life. That is why I have chosen them. Machado's "Last Night As I Was Sleeping," for example, can astound us with a completely new perspective on what we thought were "all our old failures." Neruda's "Ode to My Socks," on the other hand, demonstrates so powerfully how beauty can be found in the most mundane of objects. In pointing to the energy and power that lies in being willing to be "dumbfounded, / Unable to say yes or no," Rumi's "Zero Circle" turns the prevailing cultural creed of "just do it" around 360 degrees. Rumi's words were written eight hundred years ago, while those of St. John of the Cross, whose "Dark Night" completes the selection, were written in the seventeenth century. Yet every one of these poems speaks to our current needs and cultural moment, even as it carries themes that are eternal.

I could have placed the poems in almost any order, except perhaps for "The Journey," whose theme makes it a natural poem to begin with, and for "The Dark Night," whose peace and union are a fitting note to end on. What has influenced the order of the other poems is not so much their particular themes, but the biographical details I have included in my text. Something of my own story threads its way through the series in a somewhat chronological order, and this, as much as anything, allowed the poems to find their own natural placement.

For several years now I have recited poetry before audiences in the United States and in Europe, usually in the setting of a conference program or a church. I recite poetry of this kind because it is a way of connecting myself to the current of life that I recognize in the words, and of sharing that current with others. One way for the reader of this book to feel these poems even more directly is also to read them aloud, for then their incantatory power can ride on the air into his body. After a reading, you fall silent, and as George Steiner says, "Where the word of the poet ceases, a great light begins." At the same time, we may find ourselves understanding the poet Seamus Heaney, when he reveals to us in the last line of "Personal Helicon," that "I rhyme / to see myself, to set the darkness echoing."[2]

May these poems set free your unlived dreams; may they send a trembling echo through your bones; may they put into words what you have long felt under your tongue; and may you wake up one morning in "the new life."

1

THE JOURNEY

by Mary Oliver

One day you finally knew
what you had to do, and began,
though the voices around you
kept shouting
their bad advice—
though the whole house
began to tremble
and you felt the old tug
at your ankles.
"Mend my life!"
each voice cried.
But you didn't stop.
You knew what you had to do,
though the wind pried
with its stiff fingers
at the very foundations,
though their melancholy
was terrible.

It was already late
enough, and a wild night,
and the road full of fallen
branches and stones.
But little by little,
as you left their voices behind,
the stars began to burn
through the sheets of clouds,
and there was a new voice
which you slowly
recognized as your own,
that kept you company
as you strode deeper and deeper
into the world,
determined to do
the only thing you could do—
determined to save
the only life that you could save.

The Only Life You Can Save

"The Journey" is a poem of transformation, and as much as any poem Oliver ever wrote, it is a mirror in which you can see a reflection of your own story. It captures that moment when you dare to take your heart in your hands and walk through an invisible wall into a new life. We do not know the personal history that led Mary Oliver to the truth of this poem. Yet what matters for her, she has said in one of her rare interviews, is that her poems invite readers to find themselves and their own experience at its center. "The Journey," like so many of her poems, conjures the archetype of a fundamental human experience, and in that collective image we are each able to perceive our individual story.

"The Journey" first appeared in Mary Oliver's collection, *Dream Work,* in 1986. The critic Alicia Ostriker, reviewing that book for *The Nation,* remarked that Oliver is "as visionary as Emerson." Another critic, David Barber, writing in *Poetry Magazine,* said that "no poet has more of a claim on the title *Rapture* than Mary Oliver. . . . She is more mystic now than poet in certain respects."

When I first read this poem I had just landed in San Francisco from London. That one reading made my hair stand on end. It confirmed the rightness of all that had just happened in my life. A few months earlier, I had woken up one morning and knew I should leave my native country of England and go and live in America. Just like that. Rather than a decision, it was like recognizing something whose time had come. Everything needed to change, and the time was now. I sold my house, my library; my love of twelve years and I finally parted; I read my diaries of twenty-five years, and then burned them. I got on a plane to California, and I have been there, in a new life, ever since.

The move to America was a long time coming. I was fifty-three at the time. On the other hand, it took no time whatsoever. "One day," this kind of knowing just happens. It happens outside of ordinary time. It swoops in sideways, at an odd angle, and like the swallow, it is the harbinger of new things, a new caste of mind. I was lying in my bed in my hometown of Bath, England, when a knowing that had been gestating for years suddenly stepped out into the clear light of day. When it finally came out of my mouth, I realized that what had surfaced was the true journey of my life—not its events, the quotidian ups and downs, but its underground stream, its guiding motif.

Perhaps this sounds too dramatic, too grand a gesture, somehow, for the kind of lives that most of us live. Yet at the time it didn't feel dramatic at all. It was the only thing to do. The poem might seem dramatic, too—surely, you might think, it must have been written for the benefit of someone else; though not for you, not for your humdrum, ordinary round. After all, you may say, you are hardly about to leave everything behind and strike out into some mysterious territory.

Don't be so sure. I believe that Mary Oliver's poem can speak to anyone, wherever they are on their journey. Profound and significant changes can occur through the smallest, apparently insignificant gesture. If you are in the right place and read this poem at the right time, it may be the nudge you need to fall headlong into the life that has been waiting for you all along. It may just mean looking up instead of down; but in that shift of orientation, the whole world can change. "I turn my little omelet in the pan for God," said Brother Lawrence. That kind of omelet will taste like no other we have ever made.

> *One day you finally knew*
> *what you had to do, and began,* . . .

Everything hangs on that first step. It is not enough to know; you have to begin. Mary Oliver's great poem starts with this clarion call. The time for discussion and deliberation is over. I knew that morning that I had to do the only thing I could do. In a lucid moment like this the mind is quiet with a tender certainty. It is time to start walking, to stand by the truth you may have known all along but were not ready until this moment to call by its true name.

It had taken me a long time to be ready. In my case, the shell of my life had to be softened, broken down, even, before that moment of truth could appear. I needed to be humbled, cooked in the tears of loss, for any deeper life to emerge. It was the unraveling of my intimate relationship that provided the necessary heat. We loved each other as ever, but our lives were moving in different directions. We felt powerless to halt the drift. One day, a few months before our parting, we clung to each other like monkeys, weeping helplessly at the seeming madness of it all. Once, during that time, I came out of a hotel in Washington, D.C., just as a homeless person with a bundle on his back was limping by. I burst into tears on the forecourt, filled suddenly with the pain of his aloneness, of my own, of everybody's. How frail we all are; I felt it in the marrow that morning in D.C.

The pain of loss, grief, and despair is not essential for transformation. It is possible to step into a new life in more graceful ways. But for most of us, and certainly for me, pain and loss usually prepare the way. The moment itself may seem effortless, but a lifetime of suffering may have preceded it. A new life requires a death of some kind; otherwise it is nothing new, but rather a shuffling of the same deck. What we die to is an outworn way of being in the world. We experience ourselves differently. We are no longer who we thought we were. But I do not suggest for one moment that it is easy. Nor that there are any guarantees. If you start down a new road, you cannot know where it will take you.

All the same, when you are ready, you begin. The directness of this knowing, quiet yet strong, can propel you out of your habitual perceptions of life and into the unknown before you have even a moment to think twice about it. It is a flash from some other domain that is an intrinsic part of the human experience. Poets in all ages have caught the glimmer of it. Rilke, in one of his early poems, speaks of a man who gets up without warning in the middle of a meal

> And walks outdoors, and keeps on walking,
> Because of a church that stands somewhere
> in the East.[1]

Eight hundred years earlier, the Persian mystic Rumi said,

> Start walking, start walking towards Shams.
> Your legs will get heavy and tired.
> Then comes the moment of feeling the wings
> you've grown lifting.[2]

The church in the East, Shams, these are metaphors for the true heart of your own life. You can respond to it, or you can turn away. The forces wanting you to stay where you are can be daunting. But the choice is always yours.

> *though the voices around you*
> *kept shouting*
> *their bad advice—*
> *though the whole house*
> *began to tremble*
> *and you felt the old tug*
> *at your ankles.*
> *"Mend my life!"*
> *each voice cried.*
> *But you didn't stop.*

A journey like this goes against the prevailing current. It requires you to step out of line, to break with polite society. Other people will feel the ripples, and they won't like it. Any authentic movement usually requires a break with the past—not because the past is bad, but because it is so difficult for a deeper truth to make itself known among the accretions of habit and conformity.

It may mean that, one day, for no apparent reason, you simply know that you cannot continue to play by the rules you have accepted for years—the unwritten rules of a relationship, the abuses of power at work, the script you have written for your own life. It may signify a spiritual awakening, prompt you to enter a monastery, travel the world, announce your love for someone, or start painting—only you will know how the poem reflects the unique design of your own journey.

Whatever your circumstance, people will start to give you advice as soon as you disturb the status quo. That advice is likely to be bad. It will be bad because they are seeking, not to understand and further your calling, but to preserve the world as they

know it. Any eruption of the real into our familiar life is bound
to feel like an earthquake. Anyone who has fallen in love knows
that. And yet in the midst of the shouting and the falling ma-
sonry you will know with an unusual quietness that it is all hap-
pening in the only way it can; and that whichever way it turns
out, no matter what suffering you endure, it will be all right.
There in the midst of the cyclone is the peace that passes un-
derstanding.

> though their melancholy
> was terrible.

How many of us keep on walking, how many of us stay true to
what we know our lives are crying out for, when those close to us
implore us to stay behind and look to their needs? So much of
your life can be spent in anxiety and worry over others, espe-
cially if you are a woman. Women are both genetically and cul-
turally disposed to caring for others, even when it means
disregarding their own needs. Yet to walk on, as the person in
the poem does, is to finally realize that you cannot shoulder an-
other person's work for them. This life is a vale of soul making,
Keats said; and each one of us must take the charge of our lives
upon ourselves. Far from being a display of selfishness, this is
the most compassionate act you can do for anyone: to stand by
the truth of your own life and live it as fully and passionately as
you are able.

In leaving your past behind you, you walk through your fear
of the unknown. To walk on despite all the pleas for you to
come back is to know that you are free from the clutches of
guilt. When you are free of the grip of guilt and fear, love
blooms—love of the truth. You will say what you have to say, and
do what you have to do; not out of anger, nor irresponsibility,

but because if you do not cleave to the truth, you know you will die. After all,

> *It was already late*
> *enough, and a wild night,*
> *and the road full of fallen*
> *branches and stones.*

Already late enough: how long will you go on sleeping? This calling is passionate, urgent, even. Once you hear it, you cannot help but feel how late it is. You may have waited all your life for this one moment; there are no second thoughts. You wake to a wild night. Why does Mary Oliver insist it be wild? Perhaps because truth is wild; it is dangerous. It upsets things, brings down branches that were rotten on the tree, dislodges stones whose foundations were already shaky. It sorts the wheat from the chaff in our lives. The wild is uncompromising; its terms are always nonnegotiable, and it would rather die than not be true to what it knows. Brother Lawrence was wild in his way, tossing his omelets for God. Julia Butterfly, the young woman who lived up in a tree for two years to prevent the California loggers from hacking it down, she was wild in her way. It is always a wild ride, whoever you are, to be true to what you know in your heart in the face of the power of conformity. Like the image of transforming fire, the wild is everywhere in Mary Oliver's poetry.

No wonder, then, that a journey of this kind can seem fraught with danger, at least from the perspective of common sense. Danger and darkness are in the nature of any pilgrimage, whatever the destination. Perhaps this is why, in old Arabic poetry, travel is considered one of the four great subjects worthy of the poet (along with love, song, and blood). These were considered the basic desires of the human heart, and thus travel was elevated to the dignity of being a necessity for any human being who is truly alive. The Romans felt the same way. Plutarch tells us that before the departure of a ship in stormy weather, the captain would pronounce that "to sail is necessary, to live is not."

So when the wildness courses through your veins, you have no option but to leave conventional wisdom behind and head for the source—for the source of some holy river, the summit of a mountain, perhaps, but always to the source that is in the innermost heart. The door for this journey opens inward as well as outward, and the inner terrain is often more rugged that any outer wilderness. Inward or outward, the journey will have its own wild beasts for you to contend with. And yet from the very beginning, you will somehow be sustained by your knowing, by the rightness of it all. You will feel it in your bones. You will feel it in your blood before it ever forms into words.

Of course, conventional wisdom will call you mad enough for even thinking of such an adventure—all the more so when you start out in the middle of the night. Yet the true journey of your life *requires* a kind of madness. After all, from the standpoint of your old life, you may be throwing everything away for nothing. You do not even know what you are headed toward. Yet the first step can only ever be taken in darkness. You cannot know where it will take you. You cannot plan for this sort of journey because the entire undertaking relies on the unreasonableness of faith. Faith is unreasonable because it rests on no tangible evidence. It is beyond even belief. The person of faith does not expect everything to turn out the way they want it to; they do not expect some higher power to pick them up when they fall. Their faith is beyond belief and even beyond hope. It is a faith that comes from gnosis—the knowing that has no need of information.

Faith and gnosis are one and the same. Gnosis and truth are one and the same, and the truth is of the stars, adamantine. It sheds a different light. It is the truth that can burn through the mists of confusion, uncertainty, fear, and leave you revealed to yourself, to a new voice that was in you all along.

> *But little by little,*
> *as you left their voices behind,*
> *the stars began to burn*
> *through the sheets of clouds,*
> *and there was a new voice*
> *which you slowly*
> *recognized as your own, . . .*

However you understand it within the context of your own life, Mary Oliver's "The Journey" speaks to the birth of a new self, one not conditioned by the past. This is the self who slips through the cracks of the ordinary mind when the sentry is looking the other way. If there is one word that can describe its voice, it is the word *authentic.* It will carry your own true taste, free of the flavor of anyone else. It is true, even if small, unashamedly small. You might even say this new identity is self-born, an immaculate conception of the spirit in you that is on an altogether different frequency and level to the life you have lived so far.

You do not have to be struck by lightning to catch the sense of this poem. The reality is more likely to be profoundly simple, though nonetheless shattering. Only you will know the details. Perhaps you are walking through the park near your home, just as you have already done a hundred times, when you happen to look up, and you see as you have never seen before sunlight picking the gold from autumn leaves. In that moment, you are caught off guard. For no reason, you come awake to yourself, and from one instant to the next your life feels inexplicably different. Right there, in that park you know so well, you have entered another land, both new and somehow utterly familiar; and you have the strangest feeling: you are utterly, entirely free of everything you were, even though nothing seems to have changed on the outside at all.

This new self does not walk away from the world, but into it. Its voice, Mary Oliver tells us,

> . . . kept you company
> as you strode deeper and deeper
> into the world, . . .

It wants to plunge into life with a dedication and a commitment that can only come with a rare abandon. Not a commitment to save the world; not necessarily the determination to fight for some cause, but the readiness to stand by your deepest knowing and to express that in your life first, whatever that may mean. In daring to do that, you do not leave the human community behind; on the contrary, you affirm your belonging within it, and your identification with the struggles and joys of all.

In Japan, the Ten Ox Herding pictures of the Buddhist tradition represent the same teaching. The herder starts out, disappears altogether on his journey, and ends up returning to the world with his ox, apparently the same person who left in the first place. Everything is the same, yet everything is different. In being true to that small voice within, the poet says, you are being of service to others and to the world in the most profound way possible. You cannot know where that voice will take you, but in being willing "to save the only life you could save," you are affirming one of the deepest and most sobering truths of all: no one else can ever walk your journey for you. You alone can respond to your call.

2

LAST NIGHT
AS I WAS SLEEPING

by Antonio Machado   *(Version by Robert Bly)*

Last night as I was sleeping,
I dreamt—marvelous error!—
that a spring was breaking
out in my heart.
I said: Along which secret aqueduct,
Oh water, are you coming to me,
water of a new life
that I have never drunk?

Last night as I was sleeping,
I dreamt—marvelous error!—
that I had a beehive
here inside my heart.
And the golden bees
were making white combs
and sweet honey
from my old failures.

Last night as I was sleeping,
I dreamt—marvelous error!—
that a fiery sun was giving
light inside my heart.
It was fiery because I felt
warmth as from a hearth,
and sun because it gave light
and brought tears to my eyes.

Last night as I slept,
I dreamt—marvelous error!—
that it was God I had
here inside my heart.

Sweet Honey from Old Failures

Where do we go when we sleep? A third of our life is lived underground, and deep down inside us a stream that will rise now and then to the surface, trailing visions into our waking. Yet what if that stream had been watering us all the days of our life and we never knew it? Perhaps there is a life within life, a blessedness that pours through our days and years and we barely suspect it. This is the marvelous idea that Antonio Machado is calling us to hear in his great poem. There is another life, he says, our true one; and it is here, just below our skin and our eyelids. Sometimes we can come awake to it in our night dreams.

We spend most of our days immersed in the stories we take to be the stuff of our lives. Tale after tale of gain and loss consumes our attention for decades, often a lifetime. And then all of a sudden it is over. Machado was a man who cared little for the events of his life. He lived a plain and simple existence, much of it as a country schoolteacher. What mattered to him was the deep current that joins the human soul to the world. What mattered above all to him was to be awake to that deeper life. One of the moral proverbs he wrote in a collection dedicated to Ortega y Gasset says

> *Beyond living and dreaming*
> *there is something more important:*
> *Waking up.*

In another, he says of Christ that

> *All your words were*
> *one word: Wake up.*[1]

If we never wake up to that deeper current that is actually living in us all along, we shall end our days wondering what the flicker of our life was for, and why it didn't go out sooner. Perhaps your familiar life is the dream, and the life in you that is more truly awake must use any opportunity available to claim your attention. Sometimes the mere sight of a cherry blossom can wake you up; or, as Machado mentions in his poem "Portrait," "a garden where sunlit lemons are growing yellow." In that moment you become a "bride to amazement," as Mary Oliver says in the poem "When Death Comes." And then there are those visitations in the night. Now and then, a night dream can erupt into your life and change everything.

Six months before leaving England to make my home in America, I was awakened one morning before dawn by an image that had the quality of a vision rather than a dream. It was of a woman's face, full of presence, large eyes bathing me with a radiant smile. Her fair hair fell to her shoulders, and her face was set in a scallop shell. My relationship of twelve years was coming to an end, and the message of the image was unequivocal: Botticelli's Venus, the deep feminine, was alive and well in me and wasn't going anywhere. I need not be afraid. I was filled with joy for days, and in the ensuing difficult months, that image was a source of deep consolation for me. Despite the upheavals under way in my outer life, I was aware of a depth of belonging in my own skin that I had never felt so consistently before.

We cling so firmly to consensus reality. Antonio Machado knew this; it can seem like a marvelous error, then, he says, when an image in a night dream blazes a trail through our conscious awareness. Such images are numinous; they shine with a light that seems to have no source, like the halo around old saints in Greek Orthodox icons. They are more real, more alive, than anything we normally experience in our waking hours—though this, our true aliveness, can burst in on us anytime, anywhere—even while doing the dishes. What makes the difference is not the event but the eyes that we are seeing with.

"What have you done with your eyes?"

Machado's mother asked him this when he was a boy, and Machado carried her question, a leitmotiv, throughout his whole life, along with the associated themes of sleeping and waking. His poems are offerings of that clear and far vision. Without the gift of this kind of sight, Machado suggests in some of his later poems, we are locked in the prison of our own narcissism, unable to see beyond our own image.

We are reading this poem in translation, so the original is filtered for us through the mind of Robert Bly. We are offered in this series of images the sensibility not of one but of two poets, both of whom have dedicated their work to the uncovering of the deep soul. Bly in his own poetry and Machado in his both use images to reach the depths. No translation will ever carry the full reverberations of the original and must stand on its own merits in the new language, a fresh shoot on a foreign tree.

The original Spanish, translated here by Bly as "marvelous

error," is *bendita ilusión*. Not only is this a marvelous visitation from another world, then, but this visitation is active; it blesses us. *Bendita* derives from the noun meaning benediction. When we are awake to the life of the soul, it works on us, on our mind and on our very cells. Our jaw drops, and we are in awe before it. More than that, even, we are changed by it. A true blessing carries us from one world to another, from the world of things to the world of beings, and both of them are right here. It is all in the manner of seeing, and a blessing confers upon us fresh eyes.

Bendita ilusión Machado calls this visitation; and it is we who are blessed. Yet Bly is astute in his avoidance of the English *illusion,* which suggests something worthless because not real in the three-dimensional sense. The Spanish is closer to the Sanskrit term *maya.* Maya means not so much illusion, but trickery, in the sense of play. Now you see me now you don't. Maya is the shapeshifter. You can never grasp it, just as you can never make of the truth a fixed object without turning it into an idol. It is so beyond our ordinary understanding that we can only exclaim, "It just can't be true! It's some marvelous error!"

> I dreamt—marvelous error!—
> that a spring was breaking
> out in my heart.

You can almost feel that sensation in the chest as you read these lines, fresh water breaking out through all the old encrustations. Our habitual stances, attitudes, fears, our hurts, gather over a lifetime like layers of lime and obstruct the flow of the Milky Way that is continually wanting to pour through our heart and into our days. Your soul, after all, is not yours; it is not a property to be owned but a stream that comes through you, that flows and is never less. This is perhaps why the Buddha was silent when asked if the human being had a soul. He did not want to quantify or locate that which no word or arrow can find. It is the life and soul of the world that wants to make itself known through your particular song, deeply personal and universal all at the same time.

> *I said: Along which secret aqueduct,*
> *Oh water, are you coming to me,*
> *water of a new life*
> *that I have never drunk?*

The origin of the spring is not in your own heart; its waters are carried there by some secret aqueduct from a source beyond all your knowing. You are already joined, then, to the life of the world, even if you have not known or felt it. There, all the while, in the midst of your loneliness, suffering, and doubts—in the midst of your slumber—that stream has been coursing through you, the same one that Bly evokes in one of his own poems, the stream that

> *Goes to fill the water tank*
> *Where the spirit horses drink.*[2]

The same blessed water gives rise to poetry too, for "my poems rise from a calm and deep spring," says Machado in another context.

If you wake up and have the sensation of tasting these waters for the first time, it is because the waters from this fountain are always new, ever fresh, like the original flavor of any moment truly savored.

Now Machado takes us further into the depths of his meaning by conjuring another vibrant image, even more startling:

that of a beehive inside his heart, and of bees making sweet honey from his old failures. When I first heard these lines, they broke open my mind to a whole new way of seeing my life. I was in amazement. Imagine the possibility that every single turn of events, however dark or disappointing the outcome, can in some circuitous way be the raw material for something that eventually surfaces with the sweetness of honey. There is an ecology to our experience, Machado seems to suggest, in which nothing is wasted.

He could have followed a more familiar line, that your failures can strengthen you, help forge your character, test your mettle, as fire does steel. But he speaks here of sweetness and honey; perhaps he is looking the other way, in the direction of the heart itself. He is saying that your failures can soften you, render you more permeable to worlds you may never have countenanced if you had always met with success in the world of action. The heart, like the grape, is prone to delivering its harvest in the same moment that it appears to be crushed. The beehive in your heart is humming precisely because of those failures.

It is marvelous to consider this: everything that happens in life has its own unique and proper place, both in the ecology of a single life, and in the pattern, the web, of the human race as a whole. This is a lofty and difficult conclusion to come to, and yet it brings with it a huge sigh of relief. After all, if this is so, it means that, in the end, everything—everything—is all right. Ultimately, it suggests that whatever we may perceive to be evil has its own unique function in the whole; that in some way indecipherable to the rational mind the Divine must even include the satanic. In our personal lives, it implies a perfection in the way things are. Not that what happens is perfect, or meets our own internal standards of excellence; but that it is part of the

holographic web of a life that has its own invisible logic. As for
the meaning, it may not render itself to our conscious minds
until years after the event. In that sense, we can dare to say with
the medieval English saint Julian of Norwich and with T. S.
Eliot, who borrowed the saint's words for his poem "Little
Gidding," that "all shall be well and / All manner of things shall
be well." [3]

Of all the great teachings throughout human history, this is
perhaps the simplest and the most far reaching of all. It re-
quires

> *A condition of complete simplicity*
> *(Costing not less than everything)*

says Eliot in that same poem. It alone, if felt in the marrow, is
enough to give birth to the mystery of faith. Indeed, it is itself
nothing less than the condition of faith, which, like every image
in Machado's poem, is a spontaneous, unbidden gift of grace.

Still in sleep, still a marvelous error, Machado sees now a
third image arise,

> *that a fiery sun was giving*
> *light inside my heart.*

The sun, source of all life, springs eternal of the spirit, appar-
ently far beyond the concerns of Earth, yet the sun bathes it
ceaselessly in the light and warmth of its radiance. That same
sun Machado sees in his heart. Human heart and solar source
are one and the same. Machado becomes the source of his own
warmth and light, and in the seeing, he sheds tears. Tears of
what? Recognition, perhaps; to finally see himself in his own
true light. Tears of relief, then, of wonder, gratitude, and joy.

There is nowhere else to look, it would seem, nowhere else to go for the one who has come to this.

And yet Machado has one more step to make with us, the greatest, most marvelous error of all. He passes beyond all images finally to the source of images themselves. He dreams that God is here inside his heart. He dares to leap over metaphor altogether and say directly what he has been inferring all along: you are your own source, drink from your own well, live by your own undying light. Not the light of reason, nor of the conscious mind—this happens at night, remember—but by the light of the world that streams through your life daily. He takes the Apostle John at face value when he has Jesus say that

You are the light of the world.

That is why everything is all right. And this is the revolutionary meaning of Antonio Machado's poem.

3

SONG OF MYSELF

by Walt Whitman   *(Excerpt from the 1855 edition)*

Trippers and askers surround me,
People I meet....the effect upon me of my early
*   life....of the ward and city I live in....of*
*   the nation,*
The latest news....discoveries, inventions,
*   societies....authors old and new,*
My dinner, dress, associates, looks, business,
*   compliments, dues,*
The real or fancied indifference of some man or
*   woman I love,*
The sickness of one of my folks—or of myself....
*   or ill-doing....or loss or lack of money....*
*   or depressions or exaltations,*
These come to me days and nights and go from
*   me again,*
But they are not the Me myself.

Apart from the pulling and hauling stands what I am,
Stands amused, complacent, compassionating,
*   idle, unitary,*
Looks down, is erect, bends an arm on an impalpable
*   certain rest,*
Looks with its sidecurved head, curious what will
*   come next,*
Both in and out of the game, and watching and
*   wondering at it.*

. . . .

I believe in you my soul . . . . the other I am must not
*   abase itself to you,*
And you must not be abased to the other.

Loafe with me in the grass . . . . loose the stop from
*   your throat,*
Not words, not music or rhyme I want . . . .
*   not custom or lecture, not even the best,*
Only the lull I like, the hum of your valved voice.

I mind how we lay in June, such a transparent
*   summer morning;*
You settled your head athwart my hips and gently
*   turned over upon me,*

*And parted the shirt from my bosom-bone, and
  plunged your tongue to my barestript heart,
And reached till you felt my beard, and reached till
  you held my feet.*

*Swiftly arose and spread around me the peace
  and knowledge that pass all the argument
  of the earth;
And I know that the hand of God is the elderhand
  of my own,
And I know that the spirit of God is the eldest
  brother of my own,
And that all the men ever born are also my
  brothers . . . . and the women my sisters
  and lovers,
And that a kelson of the creation is love.*

Every Man His Own Priest

"Walt Whitman, an American, one of the roughs,
a Kosmos."   (From *Leaves of Grass,* Walt Whitman)

Walt Whitman, outrageous Walt Whitman, the wild god Dionysus returned, broad of shoulder and girth, in love with everyone and everything: Whitman is the one poet above all others who believed with a passion that the aim of poetry was to change people's lives. He referred to *Leaves of Grass*—his collected works, of which "Song of Myself" is the longest, most daring, most magnificent of all—as the new Bible, of which he himself was the secular priest. Priests of the old variety were a dying breed, so Whitman would say in his preface to *Leaves:*

> There will soon be no more priests. Their work is
> done. . . . Every man shall be his own priest.

And every man and woman shall be their own priest: Whitman's "Song" is a gateway to your own deeper identity. He turns your attention back on yourself—to the primacy of your own being, to your brotherhood with God and also with all living things. This is the 1850s, a fervent era in American religious thought when every sort of experimental philosophy and faith was being explored with enthusiasm by the educated and uneducated alike. Walt Whitman's book was distributed by a large and successful publishing house that specialized in every sort of self-hclp book. What goes around comes around. How contemporary his priestly prophecy sounds 150 years later, at the start of a new millennium. His poetic genius, his spiritual ecstasies, stretch beyond time altogether.

The line quoted at the beginning of this chapter is from *Leaves of Grass*. Whitman wanted to be known as a regular guy, and to press home the point, he had a photo of himself on the title page dressed not in the formal jacket and starched shirt of the scholar poet, the educated, sophisticated elite, but in the open shirt and boots of a working man. If it was a publicity stunt, it was also a genuine metaphor for his poetry, the wonder of which is precisely the wonder of ordinary speech and the everyday world. In the same line he calls himself a Kosmos, and his great poem is a Kosmos, too—a masterpiece of inclusion, nothing left out. To speak of his poetry is to speak of the man himself, and for Whitman there was really no distinction. Unlike W. B. Yeats, who famously said that a man had to choose between the perfection of the work and the perfection of the life, Walt Whitman wanted it all, and he urges us to want it all— to forge ourselves from our dreams.

What is "Song of Myself" if not exactly what the title suggests: a celebration of a man in the making? "The record of an artist's struggle to become himself," one biographer called it, "and also the workshop in which the change is accomplished."[1] The life and the work become one, and not just for the poet but for you, the reader, too, he hoped. In the work of reading—and as always, in the reading out loud (Whitman's rhythms will carry you far)—you may imbibe the same full-blooded joy, the same realizations, and make them your own. Walt Whitman is the poet of excess, and he can carry you far—far away, even, from who you think you are.

This is his purpose in this passage: to question our familiar identity. Who we think we are is deeply embedded in our relations with others—not only those we love, but also passersby on the street, chance acquaintances, associates. They exist, therefore so do we—in relation to them. It can even be the same with a tree or a dog, with anything that can presume to be other. I was never so struck by this as when I once walked on my own in the Sahara desert. There was not a ripple in the sand, just a vast empty expanse that went on forever without even a contour. At one point it dawned on me that with no reference point I, too, seemed to slip away; there was just the walking, with no story to tell.

Whitman summons other ways we have of situating ourselves: by the place and nation we live in, and by the effects on us of our early life. (How many of us today, in this psychological age, tend to define ourselves not only by our personal history but also by the tone of the era we are living through, or were most influenced by? (Are you a 1960s, a 1980s person, or a geek?) What we eat, how we dress, what we do, all weave their way into our image of who we are, as does the amount of money we have, health or sickness, depression or joy. All of these, Whitman reminds us, come and go; yet none of them is who we are.

> But they are not the Me myself.

Walt Whitman's words challenge conventional wisdom. After all, we are so used to considering ourselves the sum of our thoughts, actions, and feelings. Rumi, whom Whitman would never have heard of, sang the same song seven hundred years earlier:

> This we are now is not imagination,
> Not a grief or joy, not a judging state
> Nor an elation, or a sadness.

> *These come and go. This is the Presence,*
> *That doesn't.*[2]

To Rumi's glorious inwardness, Whitman adds the outwardness, the bustle of life, that was so much a feature of the urbanizing American landscape he was living in, and so much a part of the identity of Americans in any era. We are none of this, he cries.

> *Apart from the pulling and hauling stands what I am,*
> . . . .
> *Both in and out of the game, and watching and*
> *wondering at it.*

There is, he proclaims, a self that remains untouched by the affairs of the world or the concerns of heart and mind. Whitman calls it the soul. It is a companion self that looks on with "sidecurved head," full of compassion and interest, at the dramas of the personality. This self has no anxiety, whatever the personality seems to be struggling with. It witnesses and waits. It is not detached from the bodily self, in the sense of being in some other sphere; rather, it is both "in and out of the game," in the world and not of it. It is who we really are. When we know this, the tension of the game will relax.

I still remember the first time I had this sensation of being "in and out of the game." I was five or six, and I was standing alone in the London street where I lived. The street was empty. Suddenly, I became aware of myself standing there, the long rows of houses on either side of me, the darkening sky. In that moment, I felt beyond all doubt the fact of my existence, independent of everything around me, including the life story of the boy in the street. I had no words for it then, but my whole being whispered, "I am." This kind of experience can happen to us anywhere. It is both a spiritual reality and a poetic truth; and yet how difficult it is to remember that we are not who we think we are. In the Upanishads, there is a verse that describes two birds, one feeding while the other looks on. The Spanish poet Juan Ramón Jiménez said,

> I am not I,
> I am this one,
> Walking beside me whom I do not see,
> Whom at times I manage to visit,
> And at other times I forget.[3]

Walt Whitman takes us further still. These two selves are distinct yet intimately mingled; and the one is not superior to the other. Whitman is the last person to suggest that the spirit is above the body and its appetites, or that the personality is something to be liberated from. He even makes a point here to say that the one must not "abase itself" to the other. Walt Whitman is anything but a Gnostic, or a dualist: there is no more perfect heaven than where we are now. This much he makes clear in almost every line of his writing.

Purity, with its notions of ridding yourself of the lower nature, is not in the Whitman lexicon. When you attend solely to the call of the soul in you, the body and the earth are neglected as being lesser. When you lose yourself in the daily round that he describes in the poem's first section, you fall into the other extreme, and become imprisoned in matter, in appearances; then the deeper being goes hungry. Besides setting you on fire with the heat of its ecstasy, a regular reading of this poem can help you notice when you are leaning too far one way or the other. There is no greater poem for restoring perspective.

In some trial lines, written in his notebook some time before "Song of Myself," he wrote:

> *If the presence of God were made visible immediately before me, I could not abase myself.*

There is nothing, then, above or below the oneness that you are. In that oneness is everything. Far from being outside of the picture, removed from the world, God is inherent in every single atom of creation. This is a concept that has been argued for centuries. Careful, though: Whitman is not talking concepts here. His friends are known to have said that in June of 1851 he had a profound realization of the unitive state, and this poem is his homage to that.

He calls to his soul to lie down with him on the grass, in sweet pastures. He doesn't expect some message from on high, any celestial music or outpouring of wisdom.

> *Only the lull I like, the hum of your valved voice.*

The lull, the pause, the quiet caress: in that lull, the hum of the soul can be heard. In traditional music all over the world, the drone, the constant, unceasing note, has always represented that hum of the soul. In Indian music today, the virtuoso will dance in and out, up and down, all the minor scales of his instrument while behind him the tamboura player will sustain the quiet, unchanging drone. Dancers and dance master have the same relationship; so do the personality and the soul. Without the one or the other there would be no dance, no music, no life.

All Whitman's lines flow along in the present, because what matters is here, now; in this moment we are alive, not yesterday, or in some possible future. All his lines flow out of the present;

except, that is, for the ones that follow now, when he describes a June summer morning when he and his soul made love on the grass. It must have been an exceptional morning for him to refer back to it in the past tense. Erotic love and spiritual ecstasy are the same energy expressed in different ways. Mystics in every tradition have made use of erotic imagery to convey spiritual truths and joys, leaving in their wake a trail of commentators who have argued interminably over whether a mystic's words were referring to an actual physical embrace or a spiritual one. These are the first lines of the Song of Solomon, in the Old Testament (Revised Standard Version):

> O that you would kiss me with the kisses
>   of your mouth!
> For your love is better than wine,
> Your anointing oils are fragrant.

Is Solomon speaking literally or metaphorically? For Walt Whitman, there is no difference. We shall never know for sure what happened to him that June morning, though he has certainly made allusion to it elsewhere as a shattering divine experience that he felt incapable of fully putting into words. What is certain is that it was not an out-of-body experience, any sort of being raised up away from the earth into some higher dimension, astral or otherwise. What happened, happened in the body, and he describes it here as a lovemaking between his body and soul, with the soul being the active partner.

His soul plunged its tongue into his naked heart, felt his body from head to toe, and honored it by holding its feet. Seer and seen, witness and the witnessed, dancer and dance master—that June morning, the two came together as one. In that unitive condition, Walt Whitman experienced the deep peace that passes all understanding, referred to not just in the Bible, but also by all Muslims when they greet one another with *salaam*. Abiding in that peace, he knew that in reality nothing existed outside of it. The hand of God is "the elderhand" of his own, in the same way that the spirit of God is the elder brother of his own spirit. He is kin with everything and everyone in creation, and always shall be, for that is how the world was made. The tiniest part of creation—a "kelson" of it—is love. Love is the nature of all things, Walt Whitman is telling. And that is what you are: it's true! You are never for one moment set apart from the connective current of life. This is the great shout of joy that this poem sends out into the world.

4

ZERO CIRCLE

by Rumi   *(Version by Coleman Barks)*

Be helpless, dumbfounded,
Unable to say yes or no.
Then a stretcher will come from grace
    to gather us up.

We are too dull-eyed to see that beauty.
If we say we can, we're lying.
If we say No, we don't see it,
That No will behead us
And shut tight our window onto spirit.

So let us rather not be sure of anything,
Beside ourselves, and only that, so
Miraculous beings come running to help.
Crazed, lying in a zero circle, mute,
We shall be saying finally,
With tremendous eloquence, Lead us.
When we have totally surrendered to that beauty,
We shall be a mighty kindness.

Be Helpless

Rumi never wrote down a word of his poems: he would spin round a pillar in the mosque, absorbed in the depths of his loving, and words would fly out of his mouth like honeybees. A scribe would catch them on the wing with his quill. Out of his spinning, the Whirling Dervishes arose, those lovers of God known as Sufis, who would swim the mystical ocean of Islam rather than stay on the orthodox shore. Rumi, then, was a great spiritual teacher as well as a poet, and if the taste of his words has seemed to grow sweeter through the centuries and spread everywhere in the form of translation, it is because his wisdom is timeless. Rumi, the universal man, has as much to say to us now as to all those—Muslims, Jews, and Christians alike—who gathered round to hear him in thirteenth-century Turkey.

Rumi is perhaps the finest and most prolific poet of spiritual wisdom to have ever lived. His words are in Persian, a language with more layers of meaning than almost any other, and his English translators have had to sift through his meanings and settle on the one or two that English can best convey, in images that are often their own. Coleman Barks is perhaps the most familiar bearer of Rumi's gifts in English, and with good reason: his versions are honed both by a long love of the Sufi way, and by the skills of the poet that he has been since an early age. Each morning, Barks sits with a Rumi text as with some holy relic; he feels the meaning of Rumi from the inside, and it is the living kernel that he manages to deliver in his renderings.

In "Zero Circle," Rumi, via Coleman, cuts to the chase. He starts with an imperative. Why not? We either see it now or we don't see it at all: drop all pretense at being the master of your life, or you won't have the remotest chance of seeing how things really are. Rumi, remember, was whirling around the pillar, and these words fell out of his mouth:

> *Be helpless, dumbfounded,*
> *Unable to say yes or no.*

When you are whirling around like that, only one thing keeps you from falling, and it is not the you that you know. We, too, whirl through our lives, though rarely with the buoyancy of Rumi's ecstasy. Sometimes we fall exhausted on the floor. Sometimes we stay upright for years, though only because we have managed to strap a rod to our back. Better to stay on the floor, with your ear close to the ground. The twelve-step programs know this. Their first step, the foundation for all the others, is the acknowledgment that "my life is unmanageable."

Rumi is urging us not to demean or abase ourselves, but to be willing to stand there with our jaw dropped open, dumbfounded and helpless before the immensity, the impossibility, of our lives. Our jaw rarely drops because we don't want to swallow a fly. We don't want to be susceptible to unknown, unsuspected circumstances that can blow in at any moment from any angle. Except that we are, and we know we are—all the time—which is why we hang on so tightly. We stay busy, we keep our focus narrow and the windows shut.

Rumi is not asking us to cringe in a corner, to feel small, or to fall in depression because we don't know what to do or where to go. That is not the kind of helplessness he has in mind. Ultimately, these are all postures of defense in the face of the immensity. Look around, he is saying. Look at the millions of dust motes dancing. Stand there, arms wide open, and embrace the unspeakable paradox. Be dumbfounded, strung between yes and no, this direction and that, that answer and this.

When I first landed in San Francisco from England, a new immigrant in a new land, I was due to go a week later to Michigan. A foundation there had offered me a month's stay at their retreat house to begin writing my book *Sacred America*. I had spent much of the previous two years researching it, and now all that lay ahead of me was to write it down. Apart from that, my future was a great empty space—no work, no relationship, no fixed abode, and no idea. Just before I was to leave for Michigan, the foundation called me to say that they had double booked the first ten days of my stay, and that they had arranged for me to spend that time in a Christian Mennonite Retreat Center that adjoined theirs.

So it was that I arrived one summer evening at the door of a converted barn in the middle of rolling hay fields. No one was in sight, though there was a note that explained where my room was. I sat down at the desk, opened my new diary, and began to write. This is the first day of a new life, I wrote. I can do anything. I can go to a Zen monastery for a year; to Bali, perhaps; or I can start a project in Africa. Yet I knew it wasn't a matter of careful choices; I knew that my life was no longer in my hands (if, indeed, it ever had been). And at that thought, I felt a vulnerable elation. I opened my book of Rumi poems, and the pages fell open to this one.

> *Then a stretcher will come from grace*
> *to gather us up.*

In the dawn of that openness, that tenderness—and only then—something else can emerge to lift us into another, truer life. "A stretcher will come": Coleman's words suggest we are casualties, and in a way we are. We are casualties of an individualist culture still thriving on the myth of independence and self-making. Self-invention has become a kind of religion. It claims we make ourselves according to the thoughts we choose to have and the goals we set ourselves. Its First Commandment, written down many decades ago now, though still in place, is "Think and Grow Rich."

Nothing wrong with being rich, of course, and it is true that our thoughts create our experience of reality; we do indeed live inside our interpretation of the way things are. Yet our thoughts are not that reality itself, they are something imposed upon it. Reality itself is simply what is; it is neither good nor bad. It is unspeakable and irreducible either to a catalog of events or our responses to them. We are so much deeper than our thoughts, and when we step out of the ghetto of self-making (such a small neighborhood in the city of ourselves), dumbfounded not only at the vastness of the world but also at our own utter lack of comprehension of it, then a stretcher will come. It will swoop in from left field, a messenger from the other world that was there all along, and we will call it Grace, because we don't know what else to say.

I saw no one at the retreat house until lunch the next day. All meals were in silence, and I stepped quietly into the dining room to find an elderly couple eating at one end of a long refectory table. They were the Mennonites who were managing the retreat house. At the other end of the table was a vacant place setting, opposite someone else who was already eating. I filled my plate, sat down, and looked up to behold one of the most beautiful faces I have ever seen. The woman's large eyes were resting on me with a radiant smile. I looked down at my food and glanced up again. Her gaze was still on me, showering me with a direct, uncomplicated warmth. The whole room seemed to fill with her presence. I tried not to laugh. The Mennonites were eating their dessert, oblivious. I was filled with disbelief, incomprehension, and inexpressible joy.

When we fall utterly, something gathers us up. But our falling must be without reservation, without expectation, without hope, though not hopeless. You can't plan for that kind of falling. When you abandon yourself utterly to life, the river will flow and the log jam will free. *Impossible* is another word for *grace*. Who would have thought it, life takes another turn, and you are gathered up into a whole different way of seeing and being.

Maria had arrived the day before me and would be there for exactly the same ten days as me. We were the only guests. Two days after our meeting, I was looking at her out of the corner of my eye, thinking, Who *are* you? Instantly she turned and said, laughing, "Haven't you recognized me yet?" After three days, the elderly couple said they had to go away on family business; that no one else was expected at the retreat house, and they would have someone come in to fix our meals. So Maria and I were left alone in the middle of Michigan hay fields for a week.

It was not long before it began to dawn on me that I was in the company of a rare individual, one deeply trusting of the moment, who genuinely seemed to respond to everything—the cat, the housekeeper, the ants across her path, as well as to me—with an unfettered warmth and embrace. She is the sun, I thought one day. She liked candy bars, too, and came from a suburban world in New Jersey, the likes of which my prejudices had kept me well away from all of my life. Yet a spring had broken out in Maria somehow; or perhaps it had been flowing from the time she was born. She had her own original wisdom, undeniable at every turn.

Helpless and dumbfounded: that was just how I felt in that Michigan retreat house. Rumi's poem goes on to speak of a Beauty that we are "too dull-eyed" to see. In another of his poems, he speaks of going to a place beyond the dawn, to

> *a source of such sweetness that flows and is never less.*
> *I have been shown a beauty there that would confuse*
> *both worlds.*[1]

This Beauty is beyond the dawn, that is, beyond our ordinary categories of light and dark, yes and no. It is a third quality, an eternal spring, confusing to the ordinary mind, beyond its distinctions. So how can we suggest that we have either seen it or not seen it? We shall be lying, whatever we say. This Beauty is not something we can point to; it is a condition to be lived. The heroes of Stendhal's novels, especially Julien Sorel in *The Red and the Black,* find their fullness in what Stendhal calls "moments of beauty"—moments when they are utterly and unthinkingly at one with life. In that unified state, there is no one outside of the circle to comment on it. Kathleen Raine, one of England's most venerable living poets, once said to me that "beauty is the supreme value, because it is the mark and signature in outward expression of truth. . . . It is innate, because we ourselves are spiritual beings. Beauty is an experience."

All we can be sure of is that we are in the territory of the Zen koan, or impossible question. In my own case, my meeting with Maria was beyond my understanding. It rendered me speechless. The Sufis will always avoid loose talk about the meaning of existence. We are bakers and house builders, they will say. Call us for a quote. For the rest, we know nothing. Faced with the blaze of reality, with the sheer fact of our condition, there is no way to turn, except toward the core of our own being. You are, I am, that we *can* be sure of, and only that. Falling without either inflation or false humility into our own light, then, says Rumi,

Miraculous beings come running to help.

Why should this be so? Because life calls to life, and it comes running. When we are one with the life that pours through us, we are one with life everywhere, part of that living stream. Well and good so far, but Rumi hasn't finished with us yet. This being helpless and dumbfounded needs to go beyond a momentary loss of composure. Before miraculous beings come running, we need to fall apart, to unravel altogether. This is not some comforting validation of self-doubt and the personal crisis of meaning. The man who said these lines was out of his mind, crazy, wild with love and with longing. Mirabai was another wild singer-poet, hair all flying in the wind. In her poem "Do Not Mention the Name of Love"

She says: Offer your mind
To those lotus feet.

Rumi has traveled that road. He knows what it is to be crazed and out of his mind. Love does that. It takes us by the hair and swirls us around till we no longer know what our name is or what town we live in. We fall helpless in a zero circle. Like us, the zero is both everything and nothing. It is complete unto itself, the one thing we can be sure of, "and only that." This is what Hadewijch II, one of those ecstatic Beguine saints who lived in the Low Countries of thirteenth-century Europe, had to say of that same circle:

Tighten
to nothing
the circle
that is
the world's things.

Then the Naked
circle
can grow wide,
enlarging,
embracing all[2]

In this condition, there is absolutely nothing to say. We are mute, yet every cell of our being cries out with an eloquence that no voice could ever attain to: *Lead us.* In that moment, everything that we are is magnetized in the same direction. All contradictions have fallen away, and we are given utterly to that which is both in and beyond us. Rumi is calling us to that degree of surrender now, in this moment. The word *Islam,* by the way, means submission, or surrender. Rumi is addressing the very essence, not just of Muslim faith, but of Christian faith, too. Turn around, he says, step out of your mind and see who has been there all along. You will never be the same again. And how, exactly, will you be different?

When we have totally surrendered to that beauty,
We shall be a mighty kindness.

It is to beauty we surrender, and it is all or nothing, one fell swoop, even though we may have been leading up to it for a lifetime. "Mankind," Dostoevsky once said, "will be saved by beauty." It is this condition of beauty, I think, that he was referring to.

In that beauty, the soul's natural state, we shall exude a fragrance, which in past eras was known as the fragrance of sanctity. No matter how authoritative a person sounds, no matter how knowing they may seem to be, or how high their station, if that scent is not in the air, they are not quite who they say they are, or who others think they are. It is the fragrance of kindness. When the great saint Kabir died, his Muslim and Hindu followers argued over who should have care of his body. When they reached the cremation ground and lifted the shroud, there was nothing there but a heap of roses. For all the intensity of his spiritual training and practice, for all the complexity of Tibetan Buddhist ritual and initiations, His Holiness the Dalai Lama has said, "My religion is kindness." That will do for a place to start.

5

THE TIME BEFORE DEATH

by Kabir   *(Version by Robert Bly)*

Friend, hope for the Guest while you are alive.
Jump into experience while you are alive!
Think . . . and think . . . while you are alive.
What you call "salvation" belongs to the time
    before death.

If you don't break your ropes while you're alive,
do you think
ghosts will do it after?

The idea that the soul will rejoin with the ecstatic
just because the body is rotten—
that is all fantasy.
What is found now is found then.
If you find nothing now,
you will simply end up with an apartment in the
    City of Death.

If you make love with the divine now, in the next
    life you will have the face of satisfied desire.

So plunge into the truth, find out who the Teacher is,
    Believe in the Great Sound!

Kabir says this: When the Guest is being searched for,
    it is the intensity of the longing for the Guest that
    does all the work.
Look at me, and you will see a slave of that intensity.

Only This Moment

From out of the Indian subcontinent, down through nearly five hundred years, a voice has come singing whose song might easily have been written in 2001. Kabir is so contemporary it is almost strange. Here we are, in a time that more than ever before is beginning to value personal experience over the wisdom of received authority, when we are seeing long cherished hierarchies and canons of behavior—in business, in religion, in the world of ideas—being dislodged by the technology of a very new world. Here we are, in the democratic twenty-first century, when anyone can post their worldview on the Internet and generate a global dialogue independent of all creed and cultural boundaries.

In sixteenth-century Benares, there by the holy river Ganges, the young Kabir, child of a Muslim family of weavers, lay in wait for Ramananda, the great devotional Hindu saint of the day. Even as a boy, his mind was immersed in the name of God, which for him was Ram, not Allah. As a Muslim, Kabir did not qualify for Ramananda's teachings, but from the very beginning his mind was not confined by the rules of the day. He lay there by the river at the spot where Ramananda took his daily bath. When the great teacher arrived, Kabir stuck his foot out. The guru tripped over it and cried out, "Ram." Kabir took this to be his initiation, and from then on called himself Ramananda's disciple. Both Hindus and Muslims were outraged, but when they brought the young Kabir before the great master, Ramananda confirmed the boy's initiation and receipt of his grace.

Kabir was his own man. He drew from both the mystical Sufi tradition of Islam and the devotional practices of Hinduism. Like the Sufis, he married, became a householder, and continued to work, as a weaver, to support his family. When he was brought before the Muslim ruler in Benares by a Muslim sheikh, on the charge that he had made claim to divine attributes, Kabir escaped the death penalty not only by his wit, which charmed the emperor, but also because Muslim rulers, who were normally strict in such matters, tended to overlook the inspired, and sometimes blasphemous, utterances of the Sufis. Kabir is known today as an inspired poet, not only in India but also, due to the translations of Robert Bly and others, throughout the West. In his own time, however, he was a great spiritual leader first and a poet second. He was the founder of a renunciate tradition that continues to have monasteries all over northern India.

Kabir recognized no caste distinctions, none of the prescribed stages of Hindu life, and none of its six systems of philosophy. Any religion without genuine personal devotion was worthless to him. The one true religion was that of the heart, which recognized neither national nor cultural boundaries. Muslims and Hindus alike flocked to his teachings, which were orally transmitted in the vernacular through his ecstatic songs and poems. Kabir knew that one of the virtues of poetry was that it could be easily remembered. It also cut through the textual verbiage of the traditional teachings in Sanskrit or Arabic, which the ordinary people could not understand. Guru Nanak, another contemporary of Kabir and the founder of the Sikh religion, included many of Kabir's couplets in the Adi Granth, the holy book of the Sikhs.

A man may read many books before he dies and
not be a Pandit; he is a Pandit who understands
the two and a half letters which form the word
"love."

Kabir was so much his own person that he continued to gen-
erate controversy all through his life. He even made use of his
death to illustrate the blindness of following tradition instead of
listening to the call of the heart. For Hindus, death at the holy
city of Benares (also known as Kasi) leads straight to the Lord.
Those who die at Maghar, however, a town in the district of
Gorakhpur, would be reborn, according to tradition, as asses.
Despite the protestations of his disciples, Kabir, knowing his
time was near, went off to die at Maghar.

What is Kasi? What Maghar? He who dies at
Maghar is not dead when Ram has taken up his
abode in his heart. He who dies elsewhere puts
Ram to shame.[1]

At Maghar, his Muslim disciples wanted to bury his body,
while the Hindus wanted to cremate it. Kabir appeared to the
entire crowd and commanded them to lift the shroud that was
over his body. When they did so, they found nothing but a heap
of flowers. The Hindus took half of them and cremated them at
Benares. The Muslims buried the rest at Maghar, where his
tomb is now to be found in the math—the monastery of his
order, which is known as the Kabir Panth.

This poem, then, "The Time Before Death," proclaims the
essence of Kabir's life and philosophy. Here was a man who
truly walked his talk, and he is urging us to do the same.
Without even being aware of it, it is so easy to slip into living life
as if it were a rehearsal for the real thing. If you are able to take

Kabir's words to heart, you may feel the shock of living now. The truest life—the most passionately lived life—is one in which the gate of the heart is open wide to receive . . . to receive what, who? To receive the Guest, Kabir says. And who is the Guest? What does he or she look like? In the monasteries of the Kabir Panth there are no sculptures of deities, no idols to be worshipped, no pujas (devotions) to be performed. In the center of the monastery there is an open space with an empty plinth.

For Kabir, God cannot be confined to religion, to form, or to name. The Guest is a general term that each person can fill in as they wish. Yet since we know he was charged with claiming divine attributes, we might assume that Kabir saw the Guest, not as some outer force, but as the One who we truly are. Who we are in essence can be none other than that same open spaciousness, with no tangible name or form, that stands at the center of Kabir's monasteries.

To stand in that openness is not only possible now; it is, for Kabir, an imperative.

> *Jump into experience while you are alive!*

He means the experience of that openness, the presence of the Guest, which echoes in some way the theme of Derek Walcott's poem "Love After Love":

> *You will greet yourself arriving*
> *At your own door*

They both speak of homecoming, though Kabir is more urgent, more explicit; he speaks not in the future but the present tense, it's now or never for him. Salvation is not to be found after death, as most religions claim; it does not require any belief—either in a religion or in the hereafter—but it does demand that you fall down into the well of the heart. Salvation is a moment-by-moment thing; it asks you to leap the gap between subject and object, to leave behind your thoughts about your experience, which always keep you separate, and fall into the experience itself.

> *If you don't break your ropes while you're alive,*
> *do you think*
> *ghosts will do it after?*

The ropes that bind you are your beliefs and preconceptions about how life is. This is true for every level of your existence. You are more alive when you are given fully to whatever you are faced with than when you try to maintain a safe distance from it, protecting yourself from the bare reality with your thoughts and beliefs about the situation. Kabir is not asking you to throw away your discrimination, or your intuitive grasp of a situation; he is urging you, rather, to break free of your belief systems and un-examined attitudes. Whether you are on the brink of welcoming the inner lover, or in the midst of a challenging situation in your daily life, the sky will always grow bigger when you loosen your beliefs about how it is all meant to go. Nothing can be more life-changing than an escape from your own preconceptions.

There is a fatalism about the common belief that

> *the soul will rejoin with the ecstatic*
> *just because the body is rotten—*

Religions like this idea because it implies you need simply to toe the orthodox line in this life in order to receive your carrot in the next. It maintains the status and significance of religious ritual and priestly authority.

That is all fantasy,

says Kabir. Nothing but a heart on fire will get you through the pearly gates, and they are ready to receive you now, not later. That may sound all rather daunting: my heart isn't on fire, you might say. I live a quiet life, not one full of that kind of intensity—that is for poets and monks. That may be so, but it takes that kind of intensity for any human to stay in the body, even if it is burning away beneath conscious awareness. A fire you may not have noticed could be smoldering somewhere deep inside, and it can burst into flames in any moment, though always in its own time. Antonio Machado wrote a wonderful thing. He wrote:

> *I thought the fire was out*
> *I stirred the ashes*
> *I burnt my fingers.*[2]

This being human, it means carrying a fire in the breast, even if we live our whole lives going to the same job every day and mowing the lawn on Sundays. We may not feel the flame of it, but that flame is what keeps us alive, whether we know it or not. And you never know when it may burn through to your fingers. It is this, the source of our life, independent of all outer conditions, that Kabir is urging us to fall in with.

How do you do it? In another of his poems, freely rendered by Robert Bly into the current vernacular, he says

> *You will not find me in stupas, nor in Indian shrine*
> *rooms, nor in synagogues, nor in cathedrals:*
> *not in masses, nor kirtans, not in legs winding around*
> *your own neck, nor in eating nothing but vegetables.*[3]

Methods of any kind are strategies, and strategies do not open the heart's door. It has to be blown open by a great wind, the wind of love, which is the only thing that will truly carry you away. Kabir tells us to jump, to break your ropes, to plunge into the truth. This is all you can do when you have come to the end of your rope, to the end of all your strategies, and don't know what else to do. It is a surrender, a falling in; not an act or an initiative, but a willing acquiescence to what is so and has always been so. An old French prayer says it this way:

> *O lord, your ocean is so great,*
> *And my boat is so small.*

This making love with the divine, this plunging into the truth, requires what human love does—a falling away of your defenses, a recognition of your vulnerability, a willingness to acknowledge that you are on the wave of an ocean far bigger than you are. Yet in the same moment that you cry Yes! to the immensity of life, you share in its power and beauty. You are both everything and nothing. This is the great ocean that Kabir is urging you to experience, the ocean of Life that bore you into existence in the first place.

> *If you make love with the divine now, in the next life*
> *you will have the face of satisfied desire.*

What do you need to do in order to make love with the divine now? Where is it to be found?

> *Are looking for me? I am in the next seat.*
> . . . .
> *When you really look for me, you will see me instantly.*[4]

Kabir says in the poem "Breath." This present moment, not only in its external unfolding of events, but also in the domain of interior time, the time of the soul, is the gateway. This is the moment to listen for the Great Sound, the unceasing note that, through all comings and goings, all ups and downs, hums creation ceaselessly into being. And the way you reach that Sound is to travel down to the source of your own longing. It is

> the intensity of the longing for the Guest that does
> all the work.

You may not have a name for your heart's desire; you may not even recognize it as a spiritual yearning. It may be some persistent discomfort with your life that you have not known how to respond to, or some inexplicable melancholy that comes upon you some evenings and leaves the next morning. Changing jobs or marriage partners doesn't make it go away. Yet that uncomfortable itch is the raft that will carry you across the ocean. Instead of acting it out—plunging into extreme sports, wild affairs, obsessive money-making—you can allow yourself to experience it.

You can feel it, the tangible ache in the chest; you can let it carry you deeper than your thoughts about yourself, deeper than your ideas about spirituality and the meaning of life, down into the spacious simplicity, the silence that is the root of your being. Being present to yourself is the beginning of a journey without end. That kind of journey is itself the destination. All you are asked to do is to start down that road.

6

ODE TO MY SOCKS

by Pablo Neruda   *(Translation by Stephen Mitchell)*

Maru Mori brought me
a pair
of socks
which she knitted with her own
sheepherder hands,
two socks as soft
as rabbits.
I slipped my feet
into them
as if they were
two
cases
knitted
with threads of
twilight
and the pelt of sheep.

Outrageous socks,
my feet became
two fish
made of wool,
two long sharks
of ultramarine blue
crossed
by one golden hair,
two gigantic blackbirds,
two cannons:
my feet
were honored in this way
by
these
heavenly
socks.
They were
so beautiful
that for the first time
my feet seemed to me
unacceptable
like two decrepit
firemen, firemen
unworthy

of that embroidered
fire,
of those luminous
socks.

Nevertheless,
I resisted
the sharp temptation
to save them
as schoolboys
keep
fireflies,
as scholars
collect
sacred documents,
I resisted
the wild impulse
to put them
in a golden
cage
and each day give them
birdseed
and chunks of pink melon.
Like explorers

in the jungle
who hand over the rare
green deer
to the roasting spit
and eat it
with remorse,
I stretched out
my feet
and pulled on
the
magnificent
socks
and
then my shoes.

And the moral of my ode
is this:
beauty is twice
beauty
and what is good is doubly
good
when it's a matter of two
woolen socks
in winter.

The Shadow of Beauty

Pablo Neruda came out of his native Chile, as he says in his *Memoirs,* "to go singing through the world." He finally began publishing his *Elemental Odes* when he was fifty. An ode, in the original Greek, meant a poem to be sung. The Greek ode was sung so the singer could become one with the divine, and it was no accident that Pablo Neruda took on this poetic form. His odes, too, lead us toward the divine—but the divine that is right in front of our noses.

Neruda's odes are elemental indeed: elemental, of the earth; and it is the luminosity of the common world of things that Neruda reveals in these incantatory poems in which anything— anything—can serve as the touchstone for his utter delight in the fact of being alive in the physical world. Who else has written a poem to his suit, to the dictionary, to a tomato, to laziness, to salt, to a stamp album, to a ship in a bottle, to his socks? Walt Whitman, too, was in love with this world, but not even he went that far.

"Ode to My Socks" can change the way you see what is in front of your eyes. Too often, we can divide the world between this humdrum material life and some more abstract domain of meaning and spiritual significance. Neruda says no: this world and that world are one and the same. If you open your eyes and look with wonder, even a pair of socks will dance with the filaments of an invisible light.

For much of his life, Pablo Neruda served as a foreign ambassador for Chile, and during his time abroad he wrote epic poetry on the past and the present of Latin America, full of his socialist political ideals. On returning to that continent, at the height of his creative powers, at the most fulfilling time of his life, Neruda was asked by a newspaper in Caracas to contribute a weekly column. He agreed, on the condition that it would be published in the news section, not in the literary supplement. What he had in mind was a special kind of news, news of the universe—his *Elemental Odes,* in which he would bring in reports from every corner of the ordinary world that we habitually take for granted. So Neruda's odes first appeared in a weekly newspaper, bringing a precious kind of news to an audience far wider than the usual literary circles.

If you have a pair of socks that you especially favor, you might like to take them out and keep them by you while reading this poem. What Neruda is doing in his "Ode to My Socks" is bringing heaven down to earth, but pay attention, because Neruda has none of the mystical dimension of Whitman. His odes were even attacked by a Catholic priest in Chile for being materialistic, Marxist, and anti-Christian. In a way, they are. They celebrate what is right here before us, without any insinuation of some other, more spiritual realm, that stands behind the daily round. They applaud material existence, yet they do so with an exuberance and a love that would flush any pagan's cheeks with joy.

Neruda fills these socks with delight, with joy, with amazement. He pours himself into them until they literally bulge with connections and associations that join them, through the loom of his own heart, to the stars and to all the things of the earth. The material world, he cries in the lilting voice of this poem, shines forth in every moment and in every detail with its own mysterious and radiant presence. Why go anywhere else? If it's meaning you want, if it's depth, a reason for breathing, then look down at the sheaths on your feet.

Outrageous proposition! *Outrageous*—a word fitting for both Whitman and Neruda, both of them entirely without apology. Before we begin to enter the poem itself, first notice the architecture of Neruda's "Ode," how he takes us by the hand and jaunts us down the jagged staircase of the tiny lines to arrive squarely in this world with our feet bathed in beauty on the ground. All his odes have this skinny shape, just like— is it coincidence?—the shape of Chile on the map. So we cascade through the poem, we sway through it, from side to side—read it out loud, you will see. The Greek ode was set to dance as well as to music, and these far origins of sprightly step linger on in Neruda's socks.

Neruda's socks are special socks from the very first line because they are a gift. A gift has by its nature a glow about it; it is freely given, there is already a show of warmth in it, a gesture of kinship, friendship, and belonging. Not only a gift, but a gift made by his friend's own hands, imbued with her attention, her eyes, her care not to miss a stitch, her care for him. Neruda's socks are associated in this very first stanza with the softness of rabbits, threads of twilight, and the pelt of sheep. The whole world pours through these socks, we shall see; for even these humble objects, like everything else, are sewn into the seamless fabric of everything here above and below. Everything belongs, everything, and is as much a cause for celebration as anything else. How different your life would be without your socks.

Neruda slips his feet into them, and his feet are instantly transformed. They become fish, then sharks, then blackbirds, then cannons. To the deep sea, to the sky, to the menace and might of war he joins these socks. They are heavenly socks, beautiful socks; they are "embroidered fire." We are talking socks here. Perhaps you have never had a sock conversation before. Perhaps you never even thought socks to be worthy of a sentence, never mind a conversation. And here is a whole poem, an ode in their honor. Is Pablo Neruda seeing something that we do not? Is he merely waxing lyrical, piling image upon image for the sake of it? Socks are surely not worth this much consideration, let alone praise. He has to be exaggerating at best, inauthentic at worst.

I don't think so. Neruda is seeing with the kind of eye that Jane Hirshfield, a West Coast poet, had when she says in one of her poems that even the

> blown field
> of a yellow curtain,
> might also,
> flooding and falling,
> ruin your heart.[1]

Anything, as Seamus Heaney says in his poem "Postscript," can be enough to "catch the heart off guard and blow it open."[2]

No need for more than the immensity before us, if only we can be willing to free our eyes from their preconceptions, from the habitual trail of assumptions that float along with every proper noun. We can help ourselves to see anew by learning to look more softly; to become aware of our peripheral vision while looking at what is before us. We can allow a soft gaze, rather than a sharp attention, to rest on the object, knowing only that we do not know it; that—be it a piece of toast, a hat, a coin, a dandelion—it contains worlds within worlds, and a love beyond love, that have yet to reveal themselves to us. Neruda saw those socks, and his heart was blown open. Now he is giving us the fruits of the heart: his gratitude, his joy, his wonder, and humility, and above all, his love.

In that same second stanza, Neruda says his feet were honored by the socks. They seemed so beautiful, so magnificent, that he felt shy in their presence, unworthy even. His feet seemed unacceptable to him before their "embroidered fire." The socks bore for Neruda the numinous quality that fireflies do for schoolchildren, or sacred documents for scholars. Filled with such awe, such amazement, he must have found it daunting even to consider slipping them on. At one moment it seemed more fitting to put them in a golden cage and feed them "chunks of pink melon," as one would a rare and exotic bird. He resists the temptation, however, and with a certain conscience does what is required in such a situation: he puts them on.

> *Like explorers*
> *in the jungle*
> *who hand over the rare*
> *green deer*
> *to the roasting spit*
> *and eat it*
> *with remorse,*
> *I stretched out*
> *my feet*
> *and pulled on*
> *the*
> *magnificent*
> *socks*
> *and*
> *then my shoes.*

When I first read these lines, my mind skipped over their implications. The image was just one more original leap, this time from socks to hunting. Yet what is an image like this doing in a poem about socks? Suddenly, the mood is somber; death is in the air. Then it dawned on me: the whole reason for writing an ode to socks in the first place is captured in this hunting image. This is actually the very heart of the poem. Traditional peoples would always ask for the blessing of the animal or even the plant they were about to kill for food. Sacrifice is in the nature of being alive. Something has to die if we are to live. This is the deep sorrow of being cast out of Eden.

We can no longer remain in innocent wonderment of the world; we have to make use of the life of another for our own survival. The ode, the song of praise, whether to the corn goddess, to the tree, or to the spirit of a prey, acknowledges and also alleviates our deep primeval guilt. Neruda's ode is, as much as anything else, a song of expiation. These magnificent socks will eventually have a hole in the heel, and all because Neruda slips them on. He knows that if he uses them he will cause their beauty to fade into thin air. That is why he imagines what else he might do with them; anything to avoid participating in their disintegration. But what else can you do with socks, if you want to stay warm, other than put them on? with corn, if you are hungry, other than eat it? Death sustains your own existence day after day, and nothing—nothing—can make you more poignantly aware of the life in everything than this.

This is a serious poem, then. It comes with the shadow of death on it. It is also full of humor. *Humor, humus, humble*—all these words share a common root, meaning of the earth, and Neruda fills his poem with all three qualities. Francis Ponge, a poet renowned for his "object poems," said that

> Hope lies in a poetry through which the world so
> invades the spirit of man that he becomes almost
> speechless.

Like Ponge, Neruda is amazed, humbled, and almost speech-less in the face of the most mundane thing imaginable. He has looked, and appreciated, in a way that has opened a door in his chest for the world to pour through, and humor floods in on the slipstream. Poetry is perhaps more than anything else the communication of amazement before the fact of this phenome-nal world—trees, mountains, lakes, songbirds, pots and pans, doors and socks and wheelbarrows.

In the early part of the twentieth century, there was a genera-tion of poets in America who were obsessed with conveying the natural world in as objective a manner as possible. They, too, were interested in objects, but in a way completely different from that of the Frenchman Ponge, and even more different from the South American Neruda. T. S. Eliot, Ezra Pound, Marianne Moore, and William Carlos Williams had an enor-mous effect on later American poets. What mattered to them was the external object in its pristine, even scientific, clarity, not the subjective content of the poet. It was as if there was no room in the poem for the soul of the poet. The result was that in the United States, for generations, images shooting up with no ap-parent relevance from the unconscious were largely discarded, even if noticed. The unconscious was deemed either not to exist or to be an irrelevance.

Neruda, on the other hand, speaking of socks, leaps headlong into golden cages where he might feed them pink melon; into the forest with the hunters, and down into the ocean with sharks. In so doing, he opens door after door in a mansion that stretches away beyond time. Neruda gives of himself unstintingly. His responses to the socks are as significant as the socks themselves. There is a relationship unfolding in his poem, and his socks are alive with his feelings. Not just spirit, but soul, is in every line.

Neruda's "Ode" invites us, the reader, to engage with the world not just as a clear-sighted observer, but also with the whole of ourselves, including those parts that may leap out from under the conscious mind and startle us into some unimagined relationship with what is before us. When we open ourselves in this way, we become malleable, liable to be shaped by the world we live in, implicated in it, embedded in it, stained in its mud and shot through with its illumination. This is how a poem like this can change your life: it can, if it strikes you in the right place at the right time, grab you by the shoulders and pull you into the circle of living, and also dying, things. It can make you, like Neruda, a willing participant in this world, open to its pain and also its joy.

And yet, while Neruda's territory is firmly on this earth and in the tangible domain of the seen, he is, even so, a practitioner of deep sight who sets free the spirit of matter. The Good and the Beautiful are doubly so, he concludes, when form, fiber, and timeliness—"two woolen socks in winter"—come together in the matter of socks. Pablo Neruda stands square in the dappled light of this world. Perhaps, on reading his poem, you would agree with Kathleen Raine when she wrote in her *Collected Poems 1935–1980* that of all the books she had read only one remained sacred:

> *this*
> *Volume of wonders, open*
> *Always before my eyes.*[3]

"Ode to My Socks" is a page from that volume of wonders.

7

LAST GODS

by Galway Kinnell

She sits naked on a rock
a few yards out in the water.
He stands on the shore,
also naked, picking blueberries.
She calls. He turns. She opens
her legs showing him her great beauty,
and smiles, a bow of lips
seeming to tie together
the ends of the earth.
Splashing her image
to pieces, he wades out
and stands before her, sunk
to the anklebones in leaf-mush
and bottom-slime—the intimacy
of the visible world. He puts
a berry in its shirt
of mist into her mouth.
She swallows it. Over the lake

two swallows whim, juke, jink,
and when one snatches
an insect they both whirl up
and exult. He is swollen
not with ichor but with blood.
She takes him and sucks him
more swollen. He kneels, opens
the dark, vertical smile
linking heaven with the underearth
and licks her smoothest flesh more smooth.
On top of the rock they join.
Somewhere a frog moans, a crow screams.
The hair of their bodies
startles up. They cry
in the tongue of the last gods,
who refused to go,
chose death, and shuddered
in joy and shattered in pieces,
bequeathing their cries
into the human mouth. Now in the lake
two faces float, looking up
at a great maternal pine whose branches
open out in all directions
explaining everything.

Shudders of Joy

In all his poetry, Galway Kinnell digs down into the earth and finds a sustenance there that others find in tales of angels. The animal body is a standing source of wonder for Kinnell, every sinew and roll of flesh an occasion for satisfaction. I love his poem "Last Gods" because it elevates the instinctual play of lovemaking to an activity worthy of the gods and because it shows how deeply resonant our loving is with all the currents and rhythms of nature itself.

There is another reason I have included a poem as explicitly sensual and sexual as this one in a collection that claims to be able to change your life: we happen to be living in one of the most disembodied and antisensual cultures of all time. We live in a results-driven society, and our preoccupation with results is necessarily antierotic. With an anxious eye on the fast chance, it is difficult to appreciate what is before us in the present moment: the light in a woman's hair, the curve of a tree, the food on our plate. We too quickly confuse the erotic with the genital knee jerk, whereas a fully sensual life flows through all the senses to connect us to the living world in its fullness. A sensual life is a life embedded in relationships.

But we live in the most liberated society there has ever been, you might say. You can be of any sexual persuasion and find friends on the Net. Sex is for sale everywhere, and pornography is one of the great business success stories of the new millennium. Yet pornography divorces body from soul and turns the body into a thing, which can be used like any other thing for profit in the marketplace. Pornography is a caricature of the erotic; it can only exist by demanding anonymity, and substituting fantasy for relationship. Without relationship, there is no soul. There is only sensation, for its own sake; and sensation is no more than skin deep. Sensation on its own—however orgasmic—fails to deliver the goods. To skim the surface of life ultimately leaves us on our own, and predictably, lonely. One reason we seem to be such a pleasure-hungry society is that we are habitually looking for it in all the wrong places.

The Greek god Eros, on the other hand, is sensual with every breath; he likes to eat slowly, to notice the light that plays on his lover's arm, to feel the damp grass beneath his bare feet, to savor the way all things play into one another. His lovemaking is warm and powerful, not intent and angular; it is inclusive, not restricted in awareness to the body with him on the bed, but open to the shadows on the wall, the birdsong outside, the rain on the window.

Galway Kinnell's poetry is like this: it is—and "Last Gods" is a vivid example—a poetry of immersion into the fullness of experience. Not for him the ironic distance of so many contemporary voices. Kinnell stands squarely in the Romantic tradition, and if there is one poet more than any other to whom his work seems related, it is Walt Whitman. Both share not only a personal intensity but also a similar transcendental philosophy. Both explore the primal underpinnings of our conscious lives, so often disguised by cultural proprieties, and find there a living reality that others strain for in more abstract realms.

If we, like Eros, and like Kinnell and Whitman, could allow ourselves to savor more of the tangible world around us, we would undoubtedly buy less. We would buy less because a genuine pleasure is fulfilling; it is the perfectly natural and healthy satisfaction in the exchange between the senses and the surrounding world. Organic pleasure, as distinct to the trumped-up pleasure generated by consumerism, is an awareness of the passage of Eros. It is an erotic response to life, one that is physically moving. The body shudders, quivers, and trembles with pleasure. It is no accident that in Greek myth, Pleasure was the child of Eros. Yet like *erotic*, the word *pleasure* has become divorced from its original savor. We still live in the aftermath of a religion (the Catholic variety) for whom the litmus test for a sin remains the question: Did you take pleasure in it?

An antierotic culture, for all the show of freedom that seems to trumpet whatever fetish happens to take our fancy, keeps us in thrall to shame. It keeps us in the fantasy of a heaven that is not of this world, with the corollary that whatever is here below, and especially down below, needs purifying. There is something inherently wrong with the bodily life, so we disassociate from it. Sexual shame is crippling, not just of our sex life but also of life in its entirety. It disconnects us from the flow, the primal juices that give form to life everywhere. It hardens the joints, severs us from our body and our feelings, leaves a dullness in the eye. Galway Kinnell's poem can give us the confidence to know, and not with the mind alone, that the mingling of bodies can be a mingling of soul—not only of individual souls, but a commingling with the soul of the world. "Last Gods" is explicit: sexual love is, when connected to Eros, and thereby to the world, a communion with life itself.

The woman in Kinnell's poem is sitting naked, not on a bed, but on a rock

a few yards out in the water.

The man, "also naked," is on the shore picking blueberries. These opening lines plunge both us and the lovers straight into the heart of the natural world: food, water, rock, naked man and woman, all of a kind. Naked, not behind closed doors, but in the public domain, in the open air, like Adam and Eve before the Patriarchal Father God chased them out of the Garden. Kinnell's two lovers have none of the self-consciousness that is the hallmark of sexual shame. When the internal critic—the one inside who worries and comments silently on every move we make—falls away, our every gesture becomes simpler, freer, less jerky, more supple. Like these two, we will be joined to the elements, which will be able to pass through us freely like breath through a lung.

Kinnell's language here is spare, clean; every movement is sufficient in itself—she calls, he turns. But then, with an eloquence requiring no further explanation,

> *She opens*
> *her legs showing him her great beauty.*

What a simple, radiant phrase to use for that gate—the Chinese called it "the jade gate"; other Oriental cultures have compared it to the peony, while some Western artists, like Georgia O'Keeffe, echo it in their paintings of the lily flower— that gate through which each one of us has come into this world. "Her great beauty"—Kinnell dignifies and honors the vagina, that essence of the feminine which for so long, in this penis-infatuated culture, has been vilified, referred to only obliquely, or not mentioned at all.

A recent off-Broadway one-woman show, *The Vagina Monologues,* has shown just how many women themselves still feel ashamed, or at best shy, of "the great beauty" between their legs.

The show's writer and performer, Eve Ensler, collected hundreds of interviews with women of all ages and backgrounds in which she explored their attitudes to their vagina. The show's material consists mostly in her reading excerpts from the different stories, and *The Vagina Monologues* is in part a show of pride in the female sex, in part a poignant, moving revelation of the depth of shame and confusion that many women carry about their bodies.

One of the reasons why *The Vagina Monologues* has been so successful is that it has provided a forum for the public honoring of the female body, and in particular of the vagina. Women have felt validated by the show, relieved by it, brought into community through it. Even to say the word *vagina* in public turns out to have been a powerful message to the culture in general. To name something is to acknowledge its existence, which in the case of the vagina, it appears, seems to have been in doubt for more than a few members of the public. Kinnell's poem not only acknowledges the vagina, but it also exalts its beauty, and even calls it by that name.

The woman in his poem smiles, and her "bow of lips" unites the ends of the earth. Again, the person and the earth are one, which is as it should be when the person in question is open without reservation to the sensual delight of the body-as-nature. He stands before her

> > > *sunk*
> > *to the anklebones in leaf-mush*
> > *and bottom-slime—the intimacy*
> > *of the visible world.*

You can feel that leaf-mush round your own ankles as you read these lines, and that slime on the pebbles and stones and mud of the lake floor. That is about as intimate as you can get with earth and water, the oozing closeness of sludge and mush, the almost uncomfortable proximity of your amoebic ancestry. This man is about to make love, and Kinnell makes ready by joining him through all the possible filaments to the living world. By reaching down into the primeval waters, Kinnell runs the gauntlet of the mother complex, the desire to slink unconscious back into the womb; yet he keeps our head above water with the presence of the world in the form of misted berries and two swallows diving.

The man feeds his love a berry, reminding us how entwined the acts of eating and making love are, both of them an entering and being entered. Feeding another is a tender, intimate thing. There we are, with our mouth open, defenseless as a babe, while the other brings to our lips the sweetest of food. Once my lover and I fed each other a whole mango, and I realized then, as I sucked the soft, striated flesh of the fruit, that I was eating for the both of us. In the same way, when I was feeding her, I was sure I could feel the taste of mango on my own tongue as she moved it around her mouth. In that feeding, I began to sense how in service we are to each other as lovers. In being fed, I realized I was having a lesson in receiving—I took in just as much as my love decided to put on the spoon, and I received it in her time, rather than my own.

> *He is swollen*
> *not with ichor but with blood.*

Ichor: "an ethereal fluid taking the place of blood in the veins of the ancient Greek gods" *(The New Webster Dictionary).* The man is a man, not a god, so it is blood that he is swollen with. Yet these two are in paradise, in a world without self-consciousness, and so they are living and loving with the ease of the gods. Everything is unfolding in the present tense, in the eternal condition of innocence that knows no past and has no care for the future. We, the observers of their play, may be forgiven for confusing them with beings of another order than the merely human, and yet it is not so. Kinnell suggests in this poem that their ease, their beauty, is our natural human birthright.

Then he gives word to their loving in such a way as to elevate the sexuality of mouth and tongue to something approaching a holy ritual. He kneels before her, not just because she is on a rock, but also to honor her, to open her in that way. He opens her as one would a door to some ancient temple, a welcoming door that seems to smile as he draws it aside. It is a gateway

> *linking heaven with the underearth.*

Not just the earth, but the underearth—the unconscious realm of shadow and shade—are gathered up in her "great beauty," her vagina, and joined to the heavens above. Her sex becomes the center of the world, the world axis that holds the different realms in relation to one another. It is a Jacob's ladder, the supreme means of ascension and also of descent. Both, the poet seems to suggest, are necessary journeys, the one incomplete without the other. A joining such as these two lovers are starting upon is a royal road to the fullness of being human.

As soon as they come together, the world pours into the poem, frogs moaning and crows screaming, as if to remind us that when we truly make love we are never merely alone with our beloved: the world, too, is making love through us. This pair has indeed entered the temple of love; they are so wholly absorbed in their loving, so unprotected from their own instinctual reactions, that

> *The hair of their bodies*
> *startles up.*

Kinnell begins to draw his poem to a close with a final, exalted affirmation of the godly nature of this kind of loving. The cries of these lovers, he says, are not theirs alone; neither are they solely of this world. They come from a lineage both tremendous and startling. Their cries echo those last gods who once inhabited the earth, and who chose death rather than remove themselves willingly to some discarnate, ethereal heaven. They loved the embodied life, the life of the senses, and they died shuddering with joy. As they "shattered in pieces" finally, their ecstatic cries were passed on to the human mouth, to be resounded by lovers like these.

In his last image, Kinnell returns once more to the connection between earth and lovers. Who knows what happened here? Who is it that has the keys to the mystery of human loving? It is none other than the

> *maternal pine whose branches*
> *open out in all directions*
> *explaining everything.*

This knowing is not for speaking in human tongue. It cannot be contained in a person's frontal lobe. No, if you want to know the secret of love, look up into the branches of a great tree, one that holds the sky without even trying.

8

FOR THE ANNIVERSARY
OF MY DEATH

by W. S. Merwin

Every year without knowing it I have passed the day
When the last fires will wave to me
And the silence will set out
Tireless traveler
Like the beam of a lightless star

Then I will no longer
Find myself in life as in a strange garment
Surprised at the earth
And the love of one woman
And the shamelessness of men
As today writing after three days of rain
Hearing the wren sing and the falling cease
And bowing not knowing to what

Bowing, Not Knowing to What

This is one of those poems that "makes my whole body so cold no fire can warm me," as Emily Dickinson once said. Each image is so deceptively simple, the flow of the whole is so fluid, without even a pause for punctuation, that it leads me down to the end before I have quite realized the extent of the country I have passed through. What I am left with after a first reading is not so much the clarity of an understanding as the chill of a sensation. I catch the weather of the words, of their cadence, though not their fuller meaning. This is exactly what I think the American poet Wallace Stevens meant when he said that "poetry must resist the intelligence almost successfully."

Everything is in that word *almost*. Merwin does resist easy interpretation in this poem; the images are too sleek to be grasped at once by a mind that is seeking explanations. Yet they fire synapses in deeper regions, beneath the more familiar territory of the conceptual mind. The poem, like an earth tremor, leaves something shuddering in its wake. This is its transforming power. In an era like ours, so enamored of facts and sound bites, we need tremors like this. Perhaps we also need, as humankind has always done, the realization of our mortality to wake us up into a fuller life.

A second, a third reading, and I begin to glimpse the terrain more distinctly. It is my life he is summoning here, my life and yours: its underground streams; the inchoate feelings that, even unvoiced, lace their way through the events of an ordinary day. Merwin is bringing the unspoken, the half-glimpsed, the blurred shapes in the corner of the mind, into a sharper focus through the lens of his poem.

The biggest blur in our lives is surely the fact of our mortality. Few of us want to look that in the eye. I, for one—though I have thought often *about* death—have never quite thought of it this way: that in the last year, I have passed over the very day that will turn out to be the anniversary of my death. This kind of thinking brings the grand abstraction into a more concrete perspective.

Which day was it? When I first read the opening lines, the date January 31 flashed through my mind. What it means I do not know, and I am not trying deliberately to narrow my options. Perhaps some built-in protective device spared me from seeing the year as well. To have had an intuition of the year along with the day would have been far closer to the real thing. It might have turned my whole life around there and then. After all, wasn't it the mysterious teacher Gurdjieff who when asked the one thing he would do, if he could, to awaken human beings to the reality of their situation, replied that he would stamp the date of their death on their foreheads? As it is, I was let off with a shudder; at least for the time being.

If it wasn't for the poem's title, it may not be immediately clear what kind of day it was that the poet was passing over. After all, he starts with a trail of images so resonant with allusion, so evocative of different thoughts and feelings, that his central meaning is evident only obliquely: he is referring to

> *the day*
> *When the last fires will wave to me.*

What an astounding way to describe the day of your death! Think about it: which words, which image, would *you* use for that day? His "last fires" evoke for me the heat of life, its warmth and light; they continue to burn while he travels elsewhere. Life goes on, even as he leaves this earth. But perhaps the last fires are those of his funeral pyre. Yet why would they wave to him? Out of kinship? Out of love? What I do know is that his image of fire burns in me long after I have put his poem down.

Images like this one and the ones that follow do not ask for interpretation; what they *mean,* if they mean anything the rational mind can comprehend, is secondary. Their work on us, like the images of our dreams, is deeper than conceptual understanding. The potency of images lies in their ability to shape us, to set up a resonance in the imagination that may reflect in our lives perhaps only months or even years later.

Merwin's images reverberate in the mind long after we have read them on the page. His streams of shining pictures echo in some way the work of Wallace Stevens, who was a significant influence on his earlier poems. Robert Graves, the poet and mythologist, had an impact on Merwin, too. Merwin was a tutor to Graves's son in Majorca in 1950, when he was just twenty-three and not long out of Princeton. Since then, Merwin has lived in many different countries and has published nearly twenty books of translation, numerous plays, and four books of prose, as well as his many books of poetry. His is a life fully lived. He is, said Joseph Parisi, the editor of the magazine *Poetry,* "one of the most influential, most imitated poets since World War Two." This poem, "For the Anniversary of My Death," was first published in his collection *The Lice* in 1963.

> *And the silence will set out*
> *Tireless traveler*
> *Like the beam of a lightless star*

What do these extraordinary lines summon in you? Only you can know how they might set your mind alight. To me they say this: that what remains after the death of the body is a living silence; that is who we are and always shall be. The silence of our being travels tirelessly, perhaps, because it no longer has to wrestle with the resistance of matter. It can travel at the speed of light, faster than the speed of light, so fast that it leaves no trace. It is beyond time, deeper than space. Everywhere and nowhere at the same time, with the nonlocal qualities of subatomic particles. I don't know what these lines mean; all I know is that they set my bones ringing. And they leave me with the haunting suspicion that what we are after death is precisely what we are now: a resounding silence that throbs at the core of even our most difficult days.

These lines are testimony to Merwin's gift for the pulsing image. This silence that we are, he says, will

> *set out*
> *Like the beam of a lightless star.*

If the silence is a beam, it must always and already be joined to its source, which remains forever invisible, unspeakable, and completely beyond our understanding. The beam makes me think of some homing device, a kind of built-in signal or frequency through which the silence can rejoin its origins—which, in essence, it had never left. One word for that homing signal might be faith, though when I use that term I do not mean a belief in some religion, but a kind of knowing that has no external reference points. I am reminded of John of the Cross, his dark night of faith, which in turn echoes the anonymous medieval Christian text *The Cloud of Unknowing*. How else do you find a lightless star? How else do you navigate the heavens to dimensions on the other side of black holes? For these lines of Merwin come trailing dark stars, black holes, parallel universes, and all the great spaces between.

Yet Merwin is above all, as his entire body of work amply shows, a great lover of the earth and the natural world. Hardly have we set out for the stars when he brings us down to earth again. What does it do for him, this realization that he has passed, each year of his life, the date of his death? We cannot say what turned Merwin's thoughts this way. The intimation of our mortality can strike us anywhere, at any moment. But for a poem like this to be the fruit of such a realization, the knowing would have to have been a physical sensation, rather than a mere cerebral musing. It would have struck him in the marrow somehow that his life story was moving inexorably toward its final curtain.

Mary Oliver is another poet who must have felt death in her bones. The images in her poem "When Death Comes" are as concrete as you can get. The impact of death, she suggests, is

> *like an iceberg between the shoulder blades.*[1]

You can't get much more final than that. It was an iceberg that brought down the *Titanic.* You and I don't stand a chance. Our day is coming. Icebergs move slowly, imperceptibly, cutting down anything and anyone who happens to be in their path. This iceberg hits us from behind, meaning we usually don't know when that blow between the shoulder blades will finally strike us down.

What Merwin and Oliver register in every cell in their body is, see it or not, death is out there, on our tail. Think of a similar moment that you yourself may have lived, when you, too, felt the transitory foundations of your own life story. Ponder how deeply you let yourself feel the fact, or whether you moved quickly instead to some distracting busyness.

Merwin discovers it is a grace to be given a glimpse of his end. It is a grace because, as a result, he turns and sees his own life as it is now with fresh and grateful eyes. The themes of his life stand out in vivid relief. What a paradox and an irony, that we are never more alive than when we know our end is near. Death is entwined with life, and to embrace it without reserve is to embrace life with a rare passion. We are only really fully alive when we have opened ourselves to such an encounter. To watch others being killed in the movies or to be in the field as a war correspondent is to have some of that thrill vicariously. That is why violence is such a popular staple in the diet that Hollywood serves up to the public. Watching others being killed in our stead can also serve to fend off the reality of our own mortality.

The next two lines strike a chord in me as deep as any poetry I know:

> *Then I will no longer*
> *Find myself in life as in a strange garment*

Merwin's sense of impending death has catapulted him out of his ordinary awareness. Now he can fully acknowledge what "a strange garment" the whole business of life—the whole story that we play out for the duration—so often feels like. There are layers upon layers of resonance in that term "a strange garment." It might refer to the body, since we shed it at the time of death. It might point to the strangeness of being in a culture, a time in history, whose values and interests we don't really share.

Yet the term is most poignant for me when taken to refer to our identity, the story we like to tell others about who we are. To call our identity "a strange garment" echoes the same insight to be found in all those variations on the legend of the prince—the one who travels far away from his homeland and forgets his true identity. Have you ever had the uncomfortable feeling that the costume you wear does not quite fit, or that it itches under the arms? Or that you don't quite believe in your own presentation? One spiritual teacher has said that death is like taking off a tight shoe; and he didn't just mean the body. Perhaps you have felt that kind of constriction. Merwin certainly has. Ultimately, what is truly strange is the mysterious fact of being here at all, the wonder, the why and the wherefore of it.

This is why it is so common to have the sensation that we are no more than passing actors upon this earth; that we do not fully belong here. Our garments are the roles we play, and who we really are remains in question.

> *All the world's a stage,*
> *And all the men and women merely players*

Shakespeare reminds us in *As You Like It*. Then, in *The Tempest*,

> *the great globe itself,*
> *Yea, all which it inherit, shall dissolve*
> *And, like this insubstantial pageant faded,*
> *Leave not a rack behind. We are such stuff*
> *As dreams are made on, and our little life*
> *Is rounded with a sleep.*[2]

In this poem, however, Merwin is not asleep. He sees through the dream of life, and with eyes that have awoken to the fact of his inevitable demise, he realizes how deeply he has always been

> *Surprised at the earth*
> *And the love of one woman*
> *And the shamelessness of men*

He is a man of wonder, and if we were to consider our life for a moment in the light of its brief passage, we would be wonderers, too. Think of that picture of Earth taken from space, a blue ball graciously floating in vast darkness. Think of the love you may have shared with even one person. If you have not known such a love, think of the longing you may have had for it, the loneliness, maybe: how tender it is to be human! And yet how we lie to one another, how shamelessly we kill one another, or speak ill of our neighbor. That is as wondrous, as unbelievable in its own way, as the solemn turning of Earth, which never strays from its course however much commotion we make.

Then, even in the present moment, as he is writing his poem, the poet stumbles across the same amazement. He does not need some great event or affair to be staggered by the vivid presence, or nowness, of life. It is enough,

> *after three days of rain*
> *Hearing the wren sing and the falling cease*

Even the wren, the tiniest of birds, can startle us into a fuller life with its song. And what does Merwin do when he suddenly finds himself present in this way? He bows, "not knowing to what." He senses the enormity of life that stands behind this little bird's song—the heavens, the earth, all that is seen and unseen, and he bows low before that for which he has no words. In a flash of genius, he ends his poem in a gesture of humility. If he is truly embodied in his words, what else can he do, when faced with the immense open door that every moment presents us with? As much as we feel and know in this life, there are depths that we can only bow to. The one true Beloved is far beyond anything or anyone we can know; and yet not elsewhere, in some world other than this. With this final gesture, Merwin opens a door in the heart onto the trembling mystery of this world, and ultimately, onto the world beyond death. Read this poem over and over, and it may open that same door in you.

9

LOVE AFTER LOVE

by Derek Walcott

The time will come
When, with elation,
You will greet yourself arriving
At your own door, in your own mirror,
And each will smile at the other's welcome,

And say, sit here, Eat.
You will love again the stranger who was your self.
Give wine. Give bread. Give back your heart
To itself, to the stranger who has loved you

All your life, whom you ignored
For another, who knows you by heart.
Take down the love letters from the bookshelf,

The photographs, the desperate notes,
Peel your image from the mirror.
Sit. Feast on your life.

Feast on Your Life

Derek Walcott, son of St. Lucia in the Caribbean, Nobel Prize winner for literature in 1992, usually writes long poems tumbling with classical allusions, startling images, and original metaphors; long poems that often carry the tension of having grown up in two cultures—the traditional island one, and that of its British rulers. "He gives us," wrote Joseph Brodsky, ". . . a sense of infinity embodied in the language." In most of his work, Walcott carves that infinity into form with strong images like "the iron light," "the rational radiance of stone," "clouds, vigorous exhalations of wet earth."

But this poem, "Love After Love," rises from a different spring. In the simplest of terms it speaks of joy, feasting, and exuberance. It was published in a collection called *Sea Grapes* in 1976. The source of its joy is two selves greeting each other, and while it may indeed echo for Walcott himself the ultimate union of his separate cultural identities, it is without specific allusion to his own personal struggle. The language is direct and accessible, so the lines can more powerfully evoke the reader's own experiences of alienation and belonging, whatever they may be.

I have recited this poem at three birthday parties: for a thirty-year-old, a fifty-year-old, and the last for a sixty-year-old—though in the last two cases I changed the future tense into the present. On each occasion, the person for whom it was read not only recognized themselves in the lines, but also felt profoundly affirmed and validated by them.

> *The time will come*
> *When, with elation,*
> *You will greet yourself arriving*
> *At your own door, in your own mirror,*
> *And each will smile at the other's welcome,*
>
> *And say, sit here, Eat.*

How do you respond to these lines? With relief? With recognition? With puzzlement? Do you have some picture of the person you are to greet again, that you have been separated from for so long? It will be different for each one of us. Maria, my wife, recently had a direct experience of such an encounter. I woke up one morning to find her gazing into the middle distance, a light smile on her face. When I asked her what she was looking at, she said, "Myself. I woke up and saw the woman I am to become in twenty years time. She was standing at the end of the bed. She looked at me with complete acceptance of who I am now, and I felt totally loved. Her gaze made me see that everything I am at present, everything in my life now, was exactly what was needed in order to finally become her." She hadn't been dreaming; neither did she create the experience; she woke up to it.

We spend much of our lives trying to make ourselves—to create the life we want, to forge some reality from our dreams. We live in a culture wedded to the fantasy of self-determination and self-made men. Yet there is another school of thought that looks at a human life from the other direction. Instead of mak-

ing ourselves, this more ancient tradition would say we our-
selves are there in embryo from the start, and we unfurl as we
go along, colored by circumstance and climate. Just as the oak
tree is there already in the acorn, the babe carries on its brow
and in its eyes the mark and signature of its later life. Not the
details, perhaps, but the particular energetic response to life,
the quality of engagement that is unique to him. It is as if our
joys and trials are there in seed form from the beginning.

There is a Jewish story saying that when you are about to be
born, God takes you to a field covered with bundles. Each bun-
dle represents a particular set of troubles. You can choose any
bundle, but the one you choose you have to take to Earth with
you. The rabbis say that if, at the moment of death, God were
to take you back to that field and let you choose another bun-
dle with which to relive your life, you would always pick the
same one.

What may be true for the bundle of sorrows is probably also
true for the bundle of joys. J. G. Bennett, a radical English
thinker who was a close disciple of Gurdjieff, described this pic-
ture more fully when he said

> we labor under the misapprehension that we have
> to think up what we have to do. The truth is that
> this is not our responsibility, because the pattern
> of things is far greater than we can imagine. . . .
> the direct perception of our pattern belongs
> to . . . the unconditioned side of our nature.[1]

In the retreat house where I first met Maria, life showed me be-
yond all doubt how its deeper current was living me, and not
the other way around. It showed me, too, the wisdom of a
dream. On our last day there, Maria gave me a card as she was

leaving for home. We had already agreed that our encounter was so out of ordinary time that we needn't exchange phone numbers or addresses. If the pattern of life that had brought us together intended our relationship to flower, it would surely arrange circumstances accordingly. As her car left the driveway, I opened her card. It was Botticelli's *Birth of Venus*. Only then did it dawn on me: the dream I had had six months earlier of the woman's face in the scallop shell—that face was Maria's, and now, with no knowledge of my dream, she had given me the scallop shell! I wandered through the hay meadow, saying out loud to myself, "That woman is my wife!" Two years later, we were married.

The pattern of things, then, is there from the start. Who you are is there from the beginning. Your task in life is to discern that pattern, listen for it, and give room for it to emerge. More commonly, though, we are all too busy trying to make things happen—to make ourselves happen. We may push and shove through most of a lifetime before realizing that another voice is whispering beneath the fret of our efforts and strategies. I think this is what Walcott means when he says we have ignored that stranger for another. The stranger was there all along; it is the natural current of your life, which may want to go one way even as you go another. This is the current that is often responsible for the plans that seem to go awry, for the doors that refuse to open despite your persistent knocking. The same current places sudden and unforeseen circumstances and opportunities in your way. A deeper, truer life—truer to your authentic pattern—is wanting you to follow its course, except its voice is quiet and cannot easily be heard in the daily commotion.

Walcott is unambiguous: however late it may be, the time will come when the "you" you have imagined yourself to be for so long will finally greet this other "you," and both will smile in welcome. For a long or a short time in an individual life, the conscious self is liable to brook no competition—for competition is how it will view any voice but its own that arises in the mind's eye. Those whisperings in the night, the hunches, the intuited glimpses—the daylight mind will often call them deluded, unrealistic, or even the voice of the devil. Far from being the soul's executive (its proper task), the conscious self can spend many of our years assuming that it alone is the arbiter of our destiny.

When it has been ripened and softened by experience, however, it will be ready to greet the other that you are. The soul and the habitual self will be glad to embrace each other. After all, the soul needs an executive for the powers of its deeper will. Both are needed for the fullness of a human being. They are in fact so much like twins that it will be like walking up to a mirror and greeting the other there. Walcott echoes Whitman here, in the relationship of equality he sees between self and soul. Remember Whitman's lines:

> I believe in you my soul....the other that I am
>   must not abase itself to you,
> And you must not be abased to the other.

Walcott's image summons two pieces of a puzzle that finally fit together, two halves of a whole that were there from the very beginning, but at an angle to each other. Now they have swiveled to "on," and the current can flow. Walcott has struck something very deep here, a vein that is central to the human experience, the one about exile and homecoming. He is using the future tense, so while evoking the joyous feeling of finally stepping into our lives, he also acknowledges the curious sensation you may have lived with for years: that, for so long, the points of the track have not quite been in place. It is as if you have known all your life that you almost belong; that home is as close as your own jugular vein, yet still somehow elusive. That is why the one you shall love again is a stranger.

> *You will love again the stranger who was your self.*
> *Give wine. Give bread. Give back your heart*
> *To itself, to the stranger who has loved you*
>
> *All your life, whom you ignored*
> *For another, who knows you by heart.*

"You will love again": this love—this gladness at the sheer fact of belonging in your own skin—is not something new, but renewed. You were probably aware of it in your childhood, or in your teens, until it became obscured by the anxieties and preoccupations of the social self as it tried to make its way in the world. All the outpourings of Western Romantic literature have been to the other, to the beloved in the form of someone else. The Beloved, Walcott implies—and here, he echoes St. John of the Cross in our final poem—is also the one inside the cave of your own heart. This is the true sacred marriage, the union between self and soul.

I love the festival of homecoming that Walcott conjures here. "Give wine. Give bread." This is a joyous communion with yourself, with the life that knows you by heart, knows every twist and turn that you have made. It contains everything that you are, including your alienation. After all, as Rumi says,

> *Straying maps the path.*

Even the fact that we ignored this stranger for another is part of the dance. There can be no homecoming without exile, no garden without a snake. The nature of the one you gave your heart to in the interim is for you alone to know. Perhaps you gave yourself to following in your father's footsteps. Perhaps you absorbed yourself in confusion and self-doubt for a couple of decades, or became satisfied with a comfortable, though empty, life of conformity. Perhaps, as Walcott suggests when he urges you to

> Take down the love letters from the bookshelf,
> The photographs, the desperate notes,

you have covered yourself in the veil of loss and have fed on old memories for too long. Wherever you may have hidden yourself, there is always time to come out into the light of day. And that time, the poet says, is now. Now is the time to feast on your life.

10

THE DARK NIGHT

by St. John of the Cross   *(Excerpt, version by Robert Bly)*

In the delicious night,
In privacy, where no one saw me,
Nor did I see one thing,
I had no light or guide
But the fire that burned inside my chest.

That fire showed me
The way more clearly than the blaze of moon
To where, waiting for me,
Was the One I knew so well.
In that place where no one ever is.

Oh night, sweet guider,
Oh night more marvelous than the dawn!
Oh night which joins
The lover and the beloved
So that the lover and beloved change bodies!

In my chest full of flowers,
Flowering wholly and only for Him,
There He remained sleeping;
I cared for Him there,
And the fan of the high cedars cooled Him.

The wind played with
His hair, and that wind from the high
Towers struck me on the neck
With its sober hand;
Sight, taste, touch, hearing stopped.

I stood still. I forgot who I was,
My face leaning against Him,
Everything stopped, abandoned me,
My worldliness was gone, forgotten
Among the white lilies.

Among the White Lilies

This last poem is an ecstatic tribute to the deep interior passion of the spiritual lover. The idea of being in love with a nameless something inside your own heart may seem odd in our secular culture. But at the root of the metaphor of lover and beloved are two fundamental human experiences: a yearning, like some yeast fermenting beneath the skin, for a fulfillment, a completeness, that you can never quite seem to find in the daily round; and at the same time, the prior intimation of a union that you sense is already, somehow, your natural state. Longing and belonging: a whole lifetime can be defined by the tension between these two. St. John's famous poem, however, is a love song that reaches its destination; it concerns less the seeking than the joy of finding. In "The Dark Night," St. John of the Cross is yearning no longer. The mood is tender and quiet; the poet is finally at rest, for he has arrived.

All your various desires for this and that, for a better job, a more suitable mate, a more interesting life, all of them stem from this original longing for . . . Plato called it the Good; depending on your temperament, you might also call it God, or Truth, or the Beloved. We displace our fundamental wish onto concrete things because the sense world is what seems most real to us, and because we have no name for what we truly wish for.

It is so fleeting, so intangible, as to make us feel like idiots shouting in the wind.

St. John of the Cross had the soul of a lover, so his longing is directed toward the Beloved. In the manner of all true lovers, he is wholly unapologetic about the fire in his chest. All he can do is to sing about it. There is no anxiety or sense of lack in this poem. John knows with the certainty of faith that what calls him is beyond understanding and beyond all the delights of this world. If you have even the embers of such a fire in you, this poem may be a match to kindle that interior flame. Not everyone would call themselves a lover of this kind, and rarer still are those who find the union that St. John does. Yet most of us have felt the other side of belonging: a sense of lack, a longing that stirs in the night sometimes, or at the moment of waking, which prompts us to wonder whether there is more to life than we know.

St. John is willing to fall off the edge, to follow the longing down to its source. He falls deep down into its subterranean origins and discovers there a fullness that others may find in their own way through the mirror of the world, for anything we dedicate ourselves to—to a human love, to service of any kind, to an art—can lead to that same union. Mother Teresa knew what St. John did, but she found it in the slums of Calcutta. (She was in the mold of her namesake, St. Teresa of Avila, who was St. John's contemporary and great friend. St. Teresa was as active in the world as John was contemplative.)

The dedication of a St. Teresa or a St. John, though, can only come from love in the first place. It is a form of dying to oneself, a kind of self-forgetting. It is the death that Goethe points to in his poem "The Holy Longing":

> *And so long as you have not known*
> *This: to die and so to grow,*

> *You are only a troubled guest*
> *On the dark earth.*[1]

Until you come in your own way to rest in the fact of your be-
longing, you will remain a troubled guest here. How you find
the union that is the object of your restless desires will depend
on your temperament. St. John's poem is a glorious celebration
of that union. Like a song from beyond the grave (the kind of
grave that Goethe was meaning), it assures you that such a
union does indeed exist. His words are a resounding vote for
the depths of the inner life, which is rare in a culture like ours,
so overwhelmingly absorbed in externals.

He had just escaped from prison when he wrote this poem,
and some of his inspiration for it came from a few bars of a
Spanish-Arab love song he heard one night through his prison
window. While the ecstatic Song of Solomon from the Old
Testament remained the greatest influence on Christians who
spoke of themselves as lovers of the Beloved, they were also af-
fected by the example of the Muslims' long tradition of ardent
song and poetry in praise of the divine lover. The troubadours
of thirteenth-century Europe mingled with the Sufis in Moorish
Spain, and from their Muslim brothers they caught the scent of
spiritual devotion, which they translated into the more secu-
lar—though nonetheless spiritual—devotional songs of the
knight for his lady. Contemporary romantic love is a tiny stray
spark from this original fire in the heart.

St. John, writing in the seventeenth century, was one of the
last great voices to sing of this passionate love in the Christian
world. One of the reasons he was in prison was that he was un-
able to contain his fire within the doctrines of the Church. This
higher lovemaking has no need of mediating priests or even
sacraments, and one of the greatest heresies of the time was

considered to be the practice of interior prayer. As you travel down his lines, you may find challenges to some of your own assumptions about what love and passion really mean.

St. John's passion awakens in the night, which is fitting for any lover perhaps, but especially for one whose love is not of this world. John's fire was alight in the "delicious night." The night implies a condition of unknowing. We are in a land without reference points, where no one else is, and where we ourselves can see nothing. We are completely in the dark—that is the nature of this love. There is deep rest in such darkness, the kind of rest in which the conscious mind lies down quietly, and another intelligence, the intelligence of faith, can lead the way. For St. John, the dark night is synonymous with faith. The intelligence that leads the way for St. John is the fire that burns inside his chest. Poets and lovers have sung of this fire forever. It is a paradox: the fire is both a longing for the Beloved, and at the same time, a witness to the presence of the Beloved.

This burning is a precious thing, not to be psychologized, analyzed, or otherwise dampened down. It is its own special gift. If you know it, and can allow yourself to feel it, receive it without either dramatizing it on the one hand or minimizing it on the other, it can lead you by a very short path to where you want to go. This is the sweet pain that burns and is never less, no matter how many rewards we may gain in the visible world; neither our achievements, our honors, nor our successes can ever assuage this fire.

It is easy to write about, easy to speak of, but it is a lifetime's challenge to allow this fire to burn without pushing it away. I have spent much of my life romanticizing the longing and even turning it into a way of life. I was in my midforties before I finally began to acknowledge that I had been living my life as a professional seeker. The last thing a professional wants is to give up the identity of his profession. My persistent questing after some answer or salve for my feeling of lack allowed me to avoid what Rilke has called "living the question": that is, finding a solution by falling into the feeling itself, rather than leaping outside of it.

This is exactly what St. John of the Cross does in this poem: he follows his ineffable Beloved all the way down into the deepest darkness. Yet does that mean the seeking for some external answer is purely an evasion? No: the seeking has its place; not least, it can exhaust us to the point where we lay down and cry, "I don't know what to do anymore. Show me the way!" The journey is an endless paradox. The Sufis have a saying that puts it exactly:

> *If you seek Him,*
> *you shall never find Him.*
> *But if you do not seek Him,*
> *He shall never reveal Himself to you.*

I was a lover who, in truth, was more comfortable with the looking than with the finding. Like all lovers, I thought I wanted to pass from longing to belonging, from exile to home. We all want to pass from the experience of separateness to that of union. Or do we? In reality, it took me years to be willing to taste the experience of belonging, its rest; and when it eventually took root it was through the agency of a human, rather than a divine, love. The Beloved was easy to talk about, but the fire was too hot for me to simply jump in. It is often the same with the love between man and woman. Human love and spiritual love reflect each other at practically every turn, so it is no surprise that St. John's great poem was inspired by a love song that he heard through his prison window.

St. John reminds you that, when you feel the absence of what he calls "the Beloved," it is a sign that you are close, closer than you can imagine. J. G. Bennett says this, too, in his memorable book *The Way to Be Free*:

> Spiritual homesickness is necessary for us. Sometimes it remains in our heart most of the time. There are periods one goes through when one is constantly aware of being bereft of something. When this feeling comes we have to watch over our purity and not misuse it. The feeling is itself authentic and is an indication of being near to something. One doesn't really feel deprived until one is close.[2]

If you can only fall headlong into that longing, you shall find yourself where you truly belong. That is the radical cure this poem calls for. And it is as true for the love of a man or woman as it is for that nameless love. St. John is as ardent as any man would be for a woman: he wants to go into the secret chamber where the Beloved is. St. John says that his longing, this fire in the heart, led him there more clearly than even "the blaze of moon" could do:

> To where, waiting for me,
> Was the One I knew so well.
> In that place where no one ever is.

The one: St. John does not call the Beloved by name. This love has a thousand names and none. Kabir knew this, too, remember; which is why the devotees in his monasteries worship still today at an altar on which there is no image. This is the place where lover and sage meet; in the great spaciousness that contains all forms and all possible names. Whereas the sage plunges into that space by seeing into the inherent transience of all the forms that emerge in his mind, the lover falls into it through the empty-yet-full chamber of the longing heart. Both of them ultimately come to the same realization, which the Tibetans call Bliss-Emptiness, and the lover would describe by saying, "There is only love, and in love all things come to be."

For the lover, the meeting with the beloved can only take place in deepest intimacy, "in that place where no one ever is." It is no tangible place he is speaking of here, but the secret heart of hearts. And St. John emphasizes that no one can witness this meeting of lover and beloved: the lover must even leave himself behind at the door, for any self-consciousness (any "Peeping Tom") would break the union. There can be no holding back, no part of the mind hovering tentatively in the background to see how it will all work out. It is a deeply interior journey, one that requires a falling down into that fire, all or nothing. This is why St. John calls the night more marvelous even than the dawn. In that darkness, lover and beloved can become one.

How natural it is that the mystic should use the language of a lover's intimacy; for what other human experience can be closer to the merging of the individual with the Self? This is the real reason why Kabir's altar is empty, and that St. John's Beloved has no name or form: you and I *are* that Self, that Beloved; we are the one we have been looking for. *This* is the heretical message of this poem.

> *Oh night more marvelous than the dawn!*
> *Oh night which joins*
> *The lover and the beloved*
> *So that the lover and beloved change bodies!*

In this and the next two stanzas St. John echoes the imagery of the Song of Solomon, all cedars and towers and the tenderness of lovers. To cast the Beloved in the male form and by implication, himself, the lover, as female, would normally mean the marriage of the soul with Christ; yet St. John keeps the identity of the Beloved open, and makes no mention of Christ. He stretches beyond the traditional symbolism and suggests something more fundamental about the nature of the mystical lover's passion. It is not a willful storming of heaven's gates, nor a persistent wearing down of the Beloved's resistance. It is not in reality an emotional display at all or an activity of any kind. It is, rather, an actively receptive tenderness, deeply feminine in nature, which gradually refines the whole being in its quiet fire. It is a quality, not of the emotions, but of the deep heart, which has its being in silence.

Hollywood has so accustomed us to think of love and passion as heated, tortuous emotions, that the deeper stream St. John follows easily goes unnoticed. Our age, after all, is addicted to sensation. St. John is describing a state in which all the senses are at rest. He is in a condition of deep communion. Yet St. John's words are hardly lifeless, without energy; nor is the deep love of a man for a woman dull because it has reached down into the still waters of the ocean floor. On the contrary, both the lover and the saint are brimming with a deeper life stream. They have dived below excitability, even below enthusiasm, down into the deep well of Being. The Chinese poet Do Hyun Cho knew these waters. He said,

Stillness is what creates love.[3]

St. John's "The Dark Night" carries the scent of that peace and delicate tenderness, the marks of the true lover. The Beloved is asleep, and the lover is ultimately so absorbed in his presence that, struck by a "sober" wind

> *Sight, taste, touch, hearing stopped.*

This is the true ecstasy, to fall into silence and forget who you are; to be, as Rumi says it, "nothing but a head / set upon the ground / as a gift for Shams."[4] All the senses have flown away on that sober wind, the head no longer rules, and everything stops. The One Beloved, the condition of union, is to be found in the night garden of the heart, there where the white lilies bloom, there where the deep peace reigns. The white lilies: these are an Easter symbol, or picture of resurrection. In dying to the excitement and fascination of the senses, St. John is raised into the new life, that which lies beyond all explanations. To enter that stream, St. John implies, you must be willing to be cooked in the fiery silence and made more tender than you can bear. Then, on the farther side of darkness, you shall find and be found by the One you have been looking for.

Epilogue

I hope that by now you can see why any of these ten poems can have the power to turn a life around; to serve as a life raft in times of distress; to open a door in the mind when all other doors seem closed. They are a celebration, not just of the strength and beauty of language, or of the poet's art, but also of perennial values and wisdom that reach far beyond the dogma and beliefs of traditions both East and West. This is the artist's prerogative: to forge paths in regions where others are usually too cautious to tread; to illuminate depths of human experience that are somehow familiar to us all, yet which, for most of us, remain beyond the reach of expression.

Taken together, these poems can be seen and used as a primer on living life as an adventure of soul. They are mirrors for our deepest condition; they reflect our longings, our ardors, our sensuous relation with one another and with the earth; the amazement that lies in wait for us in any ordinary object. These poets are guides to be trusted; I trust them because they have tasted the fruit. Every one of these poems—including the one by St. John of the Cross—is rooted in experience, in physical sensation; that is why their flights and soarings are believable.

He that sings a lasting song
Thinks in a marrow bone.

said W. B. Yeats. These poems are of the marrow.

This world is good, they say, despite all the evidence to the contrary. They are praising poems, loving poems, singing poems, and they call us to praise and love and sing through our days along with them. They tell us we are far more than we think we are, that the power of our life lies in the choosing and the responsibility for our choices; that we alone are at the helm of our days and years. Yet they remind us, too, that there is an intelligence in life, a deeper pattern that carries us along with it, whatever our conscious choices might be. Life is a paradox, they say; you need to start walking when the time comes; yet you need to be helpless and dumbfounded, too. In those moments of giving your life over, something else can take up the reins. They call it grace.

Above all, they weave in and out of the two great themes: being awake and being love. Every one of these ten poems calls us in its own way to open our eyes to the wonder of what is around us; to the wonder of what is deep inside the human heart; and above all, to be awake to the presence, the sensation, of our own being, in the midst of all of it. Every one of them calls us to love: to dive into the fiery furnace that life really is, however that happens to show up in our particular circumstance, while not knowing how it will turn out, knowing only that whatever it is now will change and ultimately end in death. And death, too, of all life's events, is urging us to wake up and love, not later, but now.

Wake up and Love! The kindness of these poems—and the kindness of this injunction—lies in their acknowledgment that our journey happens a moment at a time; and in the end, all shall be well, whatever comes round the bend in the road. It is not as if there is some ultimate condition of presence and aliveness that we have to radiate into the world before we die. We have not blown it if our life feels like a mess, if nothing seems to be working, if everyone else seems to be making a far better job of their allotted time than we are. None of us, least of all these poets, are strangers to feelings like this. Remember Machado's dream, in which bees were making sweet honey from all his old failures.

This, in the end, is what these poems are for: far from intimidating us with some impossible standard, spiritual or otherwise, they whisper in our ear that, in this moment, we can always start over. Earth-shaking acts are not necessary; beauty and truth are there for the seeing. A shift of orientation, even in our way of getting out of bed in the morning, can be enough. (Pythagoras said, "When you get up in the morning, smooth out the shape of your body from the bed.") And if we miss this moment, it's all right, here comes another. Kabir cries,

> *Jump into experience while you are alive!*

They remind us of the deep current of aliveness that runs in our own veins. We do what we can, now, and we are only as alive, as loving and awake, as we are now. We fall often from our center, most of the time even; but here comes another opportunity, and another, and we are still breathing, and whatever happens, all shall be well. Then

> *One day you finally knew what you had to do.*

Return to these poems, your favorite ones. Read them aloud to yourself, to your loved one, to a friend; read them as often as you can. A morning ritual, perhaps, before work. Or before going to bed. Fill your heart and mind with their beauty, their truth, their deep peace. For this, finally, is the true romance of life: the romance of a soul in the making, a soul willing to fall, to rise, to fall again, in the passionate pursuit of a life fully lived. Poems like these are beacons on that path.

About the Poets

MARY OLIVER (b. 1935)
"The Journey"

Mary Oliver is one of America's most widely read contemporary poets. The critic Alicia Ostriker contends that Oliver is "as visionary as Emerson." She won her first poetry prize at the age of twenty-seven, from the Poetry Society of America, for her collection *No Voyage.* She won the Pulitzer Prize in 1984 for her collection of poems *American Primitive,* and she was winner of the 1992 National Book Award for poetry for her *New and Selected Poems.* She is a professor at Bennington College. In an interview for the *Bloomsbury Review* in 1990 she said, "I feel that the function of the poet is to be . . . somehow instructive and opinionated, useful even if only as a devil's advocate. . . . The question asked today is: What does it mean? Nobody says, 'How does it feel?'"

ANTONIO MACHADO (1875–1939)
"Last Night As I Was Sleeping"

Antonio Machado was a Spanish poet and schoolteacher whose stature in the Spanish-speaking world is akin to Yeats's and Rilke's in theirs. Machado, who was born in Seville, in southern Spain, led a quiet though deeply passionate life. His poetry, too, has the quality of being both still and passionate at the same time. His words bring both gravity and luminosity to the simplest of events and objects. His first book, *Soledades,* published in 1903, includes the dream poem in this present selection. He started his first teaching job at the age of thirty-two, in Soria, a small town in the north, where he stayed for five years. Later, he moved to Segovia, near Madrid, where he married and became more active in public life. Besides poetry, he wrote newspaper articles on the political and moral issues of the time. In 1939, three years after the start of the civil war, he moved ahead of Franco's army and crossed the Pyrenees into France, dying of natural causes almost as soon as he arrived.

WALT WHITMAN (1819–1892)
"Song of Myself"

Walt Whitman, of all poets, is America's poet. A journalist and newspaper editor in New York for some years, Whitman was interested in everything, and he was inspired by the vitality of American life and what he saw as the spiritual promise of democracy. He is known above all as the great lover of the sensory and sensual world, and his poems are a constant celebration of life on earth. He published himself the first edition of *Leaves of Grass,* his collected works, in 1855, though it took nearly twenty years and several more editions before it attracted some interest. His colloquial style and free verse emancipated poetry from the conventions of the time, and *Leaves* eventually became a landmark in the history of American letters. Whitman was deeply moved by all the issues of his time, though especially by the anguish of the Civil War; he spent much time visiting and comforting hospitalized soldiers.

RUMI (1207–1273)
"Zero Circle"

Rumi was the founder of the Sufi order known as the Mevlevi (Whirling Dervishes) in Konya, Turkey, in the thirteenth century. Though the theme of lover and beloved was already an established theme in Sufi teaching, his own poetry on the theme was inspired by his meeting and the consequent loss of his great teacher, Shams of Tabriz. Out of their relationship was born some of the most inspired love poetry ever, in which Rumi sings of a love that is both personal and divine at the same time. After Shams's death, he would burst into ecstatic poetry anywhere, anytime, and his scribe and disciple, the beloved Husam, was charged with writing it all down. Rumi's great spiritual treatise, *The Mathnawi,* written in couplets, amounts to more than twenty-five thousand lines in six books.

KABIR (1398–1448?)
"The Time Before Death"

Kabir, the son a Muslim weaver, was born and lived in the holy Hindu city of Benares. A powerful spiritual teacher, he crossed the sectarian and religious divides of his day to attract both followers and enemies among Muslims and Hindus alike. While drawing on various traditions as he saw fit, Kabir emphatically declared his independence from both the major religions of his countrymen. He is widely thought to have been illiterate, and his poems—which were part of his teaching method—were given orally and written down by others. His central message was the necessity to see through our self-deceit and recognize for ourselves the Truth that we are. Some of his couplets were preserved in written form in the Adi Granth, the holy text of the Sikh religion, while the *Bijak* of Kabir contains only works attributed to him. The *Bijak* is still today the scripture of the Kabir Panth, the monastic order that grew up around Kabir's teachings.

PABLO NERUDA (1904–1973)
"Ode to My Socks"

Pablo Neruda is widely considered the most important Latin American poet of the twentieth century, as well as an influential contributor to major developments in modern poetry. He was born in the provincial town of Parral, in Chile, the son of a teacher and a railway worker. He moved to the capital, Santiago, for his university education and published his first poetry collection, *Crepusculario,* in 1923 at the age of nineteen. *Twenty Love Poems and a Song of Despair,* which has since been translated into dozens of languages, came out the following year. Between 1927 and 1935 he held a series of honorary consulships around the world, and in 1943 he returned to Chile, soon to become a senator of the Republic and a member of the Communist Party of Chile. His political interests strongly colored the poetic output of his middle years, though his complete oeuvre, running to several thousand pages, spans a vast range of ideas and passions. *Elemental Odes* was published in 1954, and *New Elemental Odes* (which includes "Ode to My Socks") in 1956. He received the Nobel Prize for literature in 1971.

GALWAY KINNELL (b. 1927)
"Last Gods"

Galway Kinnell, an American, received the Pulitzer Prize in 1983 for his *Selected Poems.* He has been poet in residence at several universities, as well as a field worker for the Congress of Racial Equality. Robert Langbaum, in the *American Poetry Review,* said of him that "Kinnell, at a time when so many poets are content to be skillful and trivial, speaks with a big voice about the whole of life." Throughout his work, he explores his relationship to transience, to death, the power of wilderness and wildness, and to the primitive underpinnings of existence. His is an intensely personal poetry, mining the depths of his own experiences of love, fatherhood, anxiety, and joy. His work is most often compared with Whitman's, and he belongs firmly in the Romantic tradition.

W. S. MERWIN (b. 1927)
"For the Anniversary of My Death"

W. S. Merwin was born in New York, the son of a Presbyterian minister, and the earliest influence on his life as a poet was his love of hymns. On graduating from Princeton, he went to live and travel in Europe, working as a scriptwriter, a playwright, and a teacher. He now lives in Hawaii, where he and his wife have made their home on a pineapple plantation they restored together. His nineteenth book of poetry, *The Folding Cliffs* (1998), is an epic narrative of Hawaii. A main concern and theme in his work is the separation of humans from nature, and their destruction of the environment. He has also published nearly twenty books of translation, numerous plays, and four books of prose, including, in 1992, *The Lost Upland,* a memoir of his life in the south of France. In 1994 he was awarded the Academy of American Poets' first annual Tanning Prize, the country's single largest prize for poetry.

DEREK WALCOTT (b. 1930)
"Love After Love"

Derek Walcott was born in St. Lucia, in the West Indies, and after attending university in Jamaica, moved to Trinidad to work as a theater and art critic. He financed his first publication, *25 Poems,* at the age of eighteen. Much of his work explores the tension of his dual African and European heritage. His most recent book of poetry is *Omeros,* published in 1990. He is also the author of four collections of plays and was the founder of the Trinidad Theater Workshop. He has been a visiting professor at Harvard and other American universities. He received the Nobel Prize for literature in 1992 "for a poetic oeuvre of great luminosity, sustained by a historical vision, the outcome of a multicultural commitment."

ST. JOHN OF THE CROSS (1542–1591)
"The Dark Night"

St. John of the Cross was born in Old Castile, Spain, the youngest son of a silk weaver. He joined the Carmelite Order in 1563, and on meeting St. Teresa of Avila, agreed with her to initiate a reform order, the Discalced Carmelites. He was imprisoned in Toledo for his efforts, and it was in his cell that he began his work as a poet. His book, *The Ascent of Mt. Carmel,* is one of the greatest of Christian spiritual treatises to map the progress of the soul. It was written as a commentary on his poem "The Dark Night." St. John of the Cross is known as one of the greatest Christian mystics of all time.

Notes

INTRODUCTION

1. Quoted on page 7 of *How to Read a Poem*. Edward Hirsch. New York: DoubleTake Books, 1999.
2. Excerpt from "Personal Helicon." Seamus Heaney. In *Death of a Naturalist*, London: Faber & Faber, 1966.

1. THE JOURNEY

1. "Sometimes a Man Stands Up." Rainer Maria Rilke. Poem no. 19 in *Selected Poems of Rainer Maria Rilke*. Trans. Robert Bly. New York: Harper & Row, 1981.
2. Excerpt from "Unfold Your Own Myth." Rumi. *The Essential Rumi*. Trans. Coleman Barks. San Francisco: HarperSanFrancisco, 1995.

2. LAST NIGHT AS I WAS SLEEPING

1. Extract from "Moral Proverbs and Folk Songs." Antonio Machado. In *Times Alone: Selected Poems of Antonio Machado*. Trans. Robert Bly. Middletown, Conn.: Wesleyan University Press, 1983.
2. Excerpt from the poem "The Horses at the Tank." Robert Bly. In *Eating the Honey of Words*. New York: Harper Collins, 1999.
3. Excerpt from "Little Gidding." T. S. Eliot. In *The Four Quartets*. New York: Harcourt Brace, 1971.

3. SONG OF MYSELF

1. *Walt Whitman*. Paul Zweig. New York: Basic Books, 1984.
2. Excerpt from the poem "This We Have Now." Rumi. In *The Essential Rumi*. Trans. Coleman Barks. San Francisco: HarperSanFrancisco, 1995.

3. Excerpt from the poem "I Am Not I." Juan Ramón Jiménez. In *Lorca and Jiménez: Selected Poems.* Trans. Robert Bly. Boston: Beacon Press, 1973.

4. ZERO CIRCLE

1. Excerpt from the poem "There Is a Passion in Me." Rumi. In *Like This.* Trans. Coleman Barks. Athens, Ga.: Maypop Books, 1990.
2. Excerpt from the poem "Tighten/to nothing." Hadewijch II. In *Women In Praise of the Sacred.* Trans. and ed. Jane Hirshfield. New York: HarperCollins, 1994.

5. THE TIME BEFORE DEATH

1. Both quotes from *The Bijak of Kabir.* Trans. Linda Hess and Shukdev Singh. New Delhi: Motilal Banarsidas, 1986.
2. From "Moral Proverbs and Folk Songs." See Machado, above.
3. From "Breath." Kabir. In *The Kabir Book.* Versions by Robert Bly. Boston: Beacon Press, 1977.
4. From "Breath." See Note 3.

6. ODE TO MY SOCKS

1. Excerpt from "Meeting the Light Completely." Jane Hirshfield. In *The October Palace.* New York: HarperCollins, 1994.
2. Excerpt from "Postscript." Seamus Heaney. In *The Spirit Level.* New York: Farrar, Straus & Giroux, 1996.
3. From *Collected Poems 1935–1980.* Kathleen Raine. London: Allen and Unwin, 1981.

8. FOR THE ANNIVERSARY OF MY DEATH

1. From "When Death Comes." Mary Oliver. In *New and Selected Poems.* Boston: Beacon Press, 1992.
2. *The Tempest.* IV, i, 147–158. William Shakespeare. Quoted in *The Enlightened Heart: An Anthology of Sacred Poetry.* Ed. Stephen Mitchell. New York: Harper & Row, 1989.

9. LOVE AFTER LOVE

1. *The Way to Be Free.* J. G. Bennett. York Beach, Maine: Samuel Weiser, 1992.

10. THE DARK NIGHT

1. Excerpt from "The Holy Longing." Johann Wolfgang von Goethe. In *The Soul Is Here for Its Own Joy.* Trans. Robert Bly. Hopewell, N.J.: Ecco Press, 1995.
2. *The Way to Be Free.* J. G. Bennett. See Bennett above.
3. This poem was sent to me without credits. If any reader knows its source, please inform the publisher and we shall include it in the next printing.
4. Excerpt from "There Is a Passion in Me." Rumi. In *Like This.* Trans. Coleman Barks. Athens, Ga.: Maypop Books, 1990.

Recommended Reading

MARY OLIVER
New and Selected Poems
West Wind: Poems and Prose Poems
House of Light
Dream Work

ANTONIO MACHADO (in English)
Bly, Robert. *Times Alone: Selected Poems of Antonio Machado*
Rexroth, Kenneth. *Thirty Spanish Poems of Love and Exile*
Trueblood, Alan S. *Antonio Machado: Selected Poems*

WALT WHITMAN
Leaves of Grass
Mitchell, Stephen, ed. *Song of Myself*

RUMI (in English)
Barks, Coleman. *The Essential Rumi*
Barks, Coleman. *Like This*
Barks, Coleman. *Delicious Laughter*
Barks, Coleman. *Birdsong*
Barks, Coleman, and Robert Bly. Audiocassette (two tapes).
    Poems of Rumi
Barks, Coleman. Audiocassette. *I Want Burning*
Harvey, Andrew. *Love's Glory: Re-Creations of Rumi*
Helminski, Kabir, ed. *The Rumi Collection*. Includes translations
    by Barks, Bly, Andrew Harvey, Helminski, and others.
Khalili, Nader. *Rumi, Fountain of Fire.*

All tapes and books by Coleman Barks except *The Essential Rumi*
(published by HarperSanFrancisco) can be ordered through Maypop
Books. Tel. 800-682-8637. Or visit their Web site: Maypopbooks.com.

KABIR (in English)

Bly, Robert. *The Kabir Book: 44 of the Ecstatic Poems of Kabir*
Hess, Linda, and Shukdev Singh, *The Bijak of Kabir*

PABLO NERUDA (in English)

Bly, Robert. *Neruda and Vallejo: Selected Poems*
Merwin, W. S. *Twenty Love Poems and a Song of Despair*
Mitchell, Stephen. *Full Woman, Fleshly Apple, Hot Moon: Selected Poems
of Pablo Neruda*
Peden Sayers, Margaret. *Selected Odes of Pablo Neruda*

GALWAY KINNELL

Selected Poems
When One Has Lived a Long Time
Mortal Act, Mortal Words

W. S. MERWIN

The Lice
The Rain in the Trees
The River Sound
Travels: Poems
The Folding Cliffs: A Narrative
The Lost Upland

DEREK WALCOTT

Collected Poems 1948–1984
Sea Grapes
Omeros
The Inferno of Dante: A New Verse Translation
The Antilles: Fragments of Epic Memory: The Nobel Lecture

ST. JOHN OF THE CROSS (in English)

Krabbenhoff, Ken. *The Poems of St. John of the Cross*
Peers, Allison, ed. *The Collected Works of St. John of the Cross*
Peers, Allison, ed. *The Dark Night of the Soul*

Other Poets to Change Your Life: A Brief List

ROBERT BLY
Eating the Honey of Words
Morning Poems
Loving a Woman in Two Worlds
The Light Around the Body

HAFIZ
Ladinsky, Daniel, trans. *The Subject Tonight Is Love:*
    60 Wild and Sweet Poems of Hafiz
Ladinsky, Daniel, trans. *The Gift*

SEAMUS HEANEY
The Spirit Level
Seeing Things
Selected Poems 1966–1987

JANE HIRSHFIELD
The Lives of the Heart
The October Palace

DENISE LEVERTOV
Evening Train
Life in the Forest
Poems 1960–1967

JUAN RAMÓN JIMÉNEZ

Bly, Robert, trans. *Lorca and Jiménez: Selected Poems*
Hays, H. R., trans. *Selected Writings of Juan Ramón Jiménez*

MIRABAI

Schelling, Andrew, trans. *For Love of the Dark One: Songs of Mirabai*

RAINER MARIA RILKE

Barrows, Anita, and Joanna Macy. *Rilke's Book of Hours: Love Poems to God*
Bly, Robert. *Selected Poems of Rainer Maria Rilke*
Mitchell, Stephen. *The Selected Poetry of Rainer Maria Rilke*
Mitchell, Stephen. *The Sonnets to Orpheus*
Young, David. *Duino Elegies*

KENNETH REXROTH

Flower Wreath Hill
Collected Shorter Poems

W. B. YEATS

The Poems of W. B. Yeats

ANTHOLOGIES

Bly, Robert. *The Soul Is Here for Its Own Joy*
Bly, Robert. *News of the Universe*
Hirshfield, Jane. *Women in Praise of the Sacred*
Maltz, Wendy. *Passionate Hearts: The Poetry of Sexual Love*
Milosz, Czeslaw. *A Book of Luminous Things*
Mitchell, Stephen. *The Enlightened Heart*

GENERAL

Gibbons, Reginald, ed. *The Poet's Work: Twenty-Nine Masters of
    Twentieth Century Poetry on the Origin and Practice of Their Art*
Hirsch, Edward. *How to Read a Poem and Fall in Love with Poetry*
Hirshfield, Jane. *Nine Gates: Entering the Mind of Poetry*

Permissions